I0092386

ALSO BY KATHRYN REED

*Lake Tahoe Trails For All Seasons:*
*Must-Do Hiking and Snowshoe Treks*

*Snowshoeing Around Lake Tahoe: Must-Do Scenic Treks*

*The Dirt Around Lake Tahoe: Must-Do Scenic Hikes*

# Sleeping with Strangers

An Airbnb Host's Life in Lake Tahoe and Mexico

KATHRYN REED

Sleeping with Strangers:
An Airbnb Host's Life in Lake Tahoe and Mexico

by Kathryn Reed.
Published by Kathryn Reed
P.O. Box 853, Chico, CA 95927

www.KathrynReed.com
© 2022 Kathryn Reed.

All rights reserved. No part of this book may be reproduced or transmitted in any form or by any means, electronic, mechanical, photocopying, recording, or otherwise, without prior written permission. For permissions contact:

kr@kathrynreed.com

Library of Congress Control Number: 2022913382

ISBN: 978-1-952003-06-6

Front cover photo © ediebloom.
Back cover photos © Kathryn Reed.
Author photo © Tim Parsons.
Cover design by Joann Eisenbrandt.

# To AJ,
# The best co-host

# Contents

# Introduction

Living on the property as an Airbnb host means cohabitating with people who are neither friend nor family. As paid guests in my home, it put them into an entirely different category, one I never imagined because of how much I like my privacy. They were strangers paying to sleep in my home. Through my two listings I met incredible people with whom I shared a drink or two. I also had experiences I would rather not repeat, like when the police were involved, or when I used a hammer to knock a hole in the door to access the rented bedroom because I had no idea, after years of living in the house, that the door had a lock on it.

At times it felt like friends were in the house—not new friends, but people I had known for years. This was comforting. It made me secure in my decision to open my home to people I did not know. Then there were the times when a single night felt like an eternity, when I wanted to get a hotel room to get away from the unwanted guests down the hall. On those occasions I was ready to abandon the whole hosting venture. The stress and inconvenience had me questioning whether it made sense to keep a house that no longer felt like home.

Needing to find a way to pay the entire mortgage after ending a twelve-year relationship led me to become an Airbnb host. I would have preferred the house be occupied by just me and my dog, AJ, but I knew I needed a cushion when it came to income. Hosting had to be better than settling for one of the rentals I had looked at, especially considering they cost as much as the house payment. A full-time roommate was a hard no for so many reasons. At least with Airbnb I reasoned any troublesome guests would have a check-out date, which would not have been the scenario with someone who lived with me all the time. I also thought this hosting gig would be a great way to meet travelers, to live vicariously through them. Ultimately, though, being a host became more of a business transaction than a social encounter. This made sense considering the impetus for being a host was rooted in wanting to make money.

South Lake Tahoe, California, was an ideal location for such an endeavor because so many people who visit this mountain town are a short drive from the San Francisco Bay Area as well as from the Sacramento region. Northern California is the primary tourism market for the entire Tahoe-Truckee region. Lake Tahoe is also a year-round destination for people from all over the world, meaning the potential for this to be a successful enterprise was even greater by not having to solely rely on people driving from their home to mine. My gamble paid off starting in spring 2015. I rented out the primary bedroom until early 2018, at which time I put the house up for sale. In fall 2018, I was back in the Airbnb hosting business at my sister and brother-in-law's place in Todos Santos, Mexico, which is about an hour north of Cabo San Lucas on the Pacific Ocean side of Baja California Sur. I did this for two winter seasons.

My two listings were extremely different. In South Lake Tahoe I gave people the primary bedroom, which included a private bathroom. It was considered a shared house, with guests having their own room. More than one person commented on the super comfortable king-size bed; with some Europeans saying they had never seen such a large bed. The dresser and closet were practically empty as I kept my belongings in the guest room. This gave me a sense of never quite having the house to myself even when I was alone because I was living out of two rooms. The "traditional" guest room is where I went when paying guests were in the house. We shared the living room and hot tub, though usually not at the same time. They could use the refrigerator and microwave but were not permitted to do any real cooking because I am a vegetarian. I did not want meat or fish on my pans, utensils, or dishes. Nor did I want the smell of meat in the house. Friends suggested providing a dormitory-size fridge for guests so they would have less need to venture from their room and it would be one less thing I would have to share. People did not bring much food and rarely had leftovers so the refrigerator space was no big deal. No one balked at having to walk down the hall if they wanted something from the refrigerator. If people ate any of my food without asking, I never noticed. Money was the biggest deterrent for not putting a refrigerator in the Airbnb room. I had no desire to make substantive investments in this venture before I knew I would want to keep doing it. Once guests proved the main fridge was no big deal, I did not give a mini-personalized one another thought.

In Mexico, people had the entire downstairs, which included two bedrooms, each with a queen bed. They shared a full bath. The kitchen was theirs, as was the living room and outdoor dining table that sat eight. The entire space was plenty big enough for four people. They were welcome to venture upstairs to enjoy the deck for sunning, whale watching or hanging out. It was the perfect place to view the sun disappearing into the ocean and then the spectacular colors dancing across the Sierra de la Laguna mountain range to the east. The house was the perfect setup for Airbnb because we each had our own entrances. While the house was two stories, the stairs were outside at the back patio. Guests only had to be upstairs if they wanted to enjoy the views.

Having listings in diverse locations with extremely different setups meant the clientele also varied. Most guests coming to-

Lake Tahoe were from Northern California, while Mexico guests were primarily from throughout the West Coast of the United States. Tahoe visitors predominantly came on the weekends, with a single night not uncommon. In Mexico, stays were longer; usually five days. In Tahoe, it was a mix of Caucasians and Asians who visited, while in Mexico it was primarily Caucasians. Both locales attracted a healthy dose of those in their thirties, forties and fifties. However, the Tahoe room saw a fair share of those in their twenties. In Mexico, the age went up into the sixties and older. I understood the length of stays—easy to drive for a weekend to Tahoe; flying takes more effort so to make it worthwhile a longer trip was the norm. Younger people often have less money and time off, so going to Tahoe was easy and could be cheap. Thirteen days was the longest anyone stayed in Mexico, a long weekend was usually the maximum in Lake Tahoe.

Once I was set up all I needed was people to start booking my place. I cheated a bit as a new host. I knew reviews were essential; they are an attribute of Airbnb that I liked as a host and still like as a guest. Writing a review is not mandatory, but receiving one is essential to hosts and future guests. Without reviews—and positive ones—it is hard to get bookings or for hosts to want to hit the "approve" button. My initial reviews as a host at both locations were bogus. I had someone book a stay, then write a review. It was a small investment on my part to get my short-term rental business off the ground. The cost to me was refunding my "guests" the fees Airbnb charged them and absorbing what the company took from me as a host. "My guest" had been to both places, so what the person wrote was the truth. That person just had never actually been an Airbnb guest at those locations. I looked at these reviews as conversation starters. They worked. Bookings came in quickly in Tahoe, with authentic reviews following. Mexico guests were slower to come, which in part had to do with starting in the early fall when it was still hot and humid. A friend who had visited Todos Santos offered to write a review as well, so that meant having two not truly authentic reviews for that property. From then on it was all paid guests who left their opinions.

Literally getting guests into the house took some thought. Leaving a key under the mat did not seem logical or safe. In Tahoe I installed a lock box so travelers would be able to get a key when I was not there. Surprisingly, no one ever misplaced it. In Mexico, my sister installed a keyless entry on the front door. This way guests only had to remember a simple code, which often was the last four digits of their phone number. This is the route I would go in the future because of ease for everyone, well, most everyone. There was the one guy who said he did not receive the code even though the string of emails proved otherwise. He had a hard time remembering the code was his phone number.

Before becoming a host, I had never used Airbnb as a guest. My knowledge of the company was from friends and family, and what I had read. My lack of personal experience with this short-term rental startup that ballooned into a billion-dollar publicly traded company was not going to stop me from going forward as a host, even though some people in my circle were not convinced this was a well-thought-out idea. They were right, it was not well thought out. But so many of my major life decisions have been more spontaneous than well researched. That approach has served me well. To me, this quasi-business adventure was my best option. I would deal with the consequences as they arose.

The humble and humorous beginning of the company, and the fact it was much more than "McMansions" that were available on the platform had me believing Airbnb was where I should list my room in South Lake Tahoe. I knew of no other company that allowed a person to rent out only a room as opposed to a whole house. In 2015, whole house rentals were the norm in the short-term rental industry. Airbnb was founded by Brian Chesky, Joe Gebbia, and Nate Blecharczyk in 2008 in San Francisco. It has grown to include six million listings run by more than four million hosts in more than one-hundred thousand cities, and in more than two hundred countries. Some rentals are similar to what I had, others are castles, while a hammock is also among the choices. The accommodations are limited by a host's imagination and a traveler's desire. Today, people have second, third and fourth homes as listings, making Airbnb a huge source of their income. Even though the company's cash flow was interrupted in 2020 when people stopped traveling because of the COVID-19 pandemic, not everyone abided by the stay-at-home orders issued by cities and states. Travel never completely ceased.

Early on the company became a huge disrupter in the world of traditional lodging. It gave people the opportunity to live like a local in a house, condo or apartment in residential areas. This created its own set of problems, and eventually led to cottage industries that focused on helping municipalities crack down on rowdy renters, and hosts who were negligent about paying taxes and permitting fees. Airbnb hosts compete against everyone else who is doing the short-term rental gig, as well as hotels and other lodging establishments. Once transient occupancy taxes started to be collected, it put all short-term rentals on an even playing field. Prior to this, traditional lodging operators complained that people like me were playing by a different set of rules by not having to pay transient occupancy taxes. They thought guests would want to stay where they did not have to pay a tax. I could not convince them I was attracting a different client than they were going after. South Lake Tahoe hosts eventually had to pay the lodging tax to the city on a quarterly basis. While hosting in Mexico, Airbnb started to collect the tax directly from the renter at the time of booking and then transferred it to the government. The latter was a more seamless transaction from a host's perspective, and ensured the correct amount of money that was owed reached the appropriate entity.

In the end, I put a few bucks in the bank from the Tahoe house, though never as much as I had hoped. In Mexico I helped defray the expense of a second home for my relatives. The money I collected in Todos Santos was transferred to my sister's account. Our deal was I could live rent free in exchange for running the Airbnb operation. Airbnb income all depends on what one charges per night and the number of nights booked, which is the same business model as any lodging property. It is possible to have a different price for every night. I used the same practice hotels employ by raising rates during holiday periods. During the second winter in Mexico I upped the price on weekends as well, which did not adversely affect bookings. I wish I would have employed the same philosophy in South Lake Tahoe.

When I started using Airbnb as a guest I was cognizant of wanting to be respectful, knowing that I was in someone's home whether they were there or not. I treat an Airbnb rental differently than I do a hotel. I am not saying this is a good thing. Just reality. At an Airbnb I do not take excessively long showers, use of electricity is within reason, and I pay attention to my cleanliness. I turn lights off when I leave my hotel room, but while I am in the room the thermostat is set so I am comfortable. I do not like to waste water, but I love long showers. Hotels are not going to rate me on my cleanliness. I am not a slob, but I will leave dirty wine glasses on a counter, whereas anywhere else I wash them. At a hotel, the bathroom always looks like it was used, whereas at a house rental I wipe the counter, and make sure no toothpaste is in the sink.

Until I got into the short-term rental business, I had no idea how clean or dirty people could be. Most made the bed. I found this silly since they knew I would be washing the sheets. Maybe they thought on the reviews they would get a lower rating on the cleanliness question if they did not make it. A few stripped the bed. This was welcome, but always surprised me. I never let the status of the bed be criteria in my cleanliness rating except for the condom incident.

It says something about a person who opens their home to strangers, just as it says something about people who willingly pay to stay with someone they do not know. What it says, well, that is for you to decide.

CHAPTER ONE

# A Rocky Start

## Nervous Beginnings

My first request from real guests was for the three nights of Memorial Day weekend 2015. This couple had no reviews because they were new to Airbnb. As a newbie myself to this whole shared economy gig I had to take my chances. Before the first guests arrived, a friend told me to lock my bedroom door at night. I smiled, not revealing no lock existed. My ex left me pepper spray in case strangers came wandering in. I was always afraid I would spray the dog or myself, thus potentially putting us in greater danger. Good thing I never felt the need to use it.

Other friends said be sure to vet the guests thoroughly. I assured them I would while secretly knowing that was never going to happen. They knew I had years of screening potential massage clients, and that as a journalist my interview skills were sharp. They thought all of that would somehow equip me for this new venture. The reality is I had no idea how to check out the Airbnb'ers. With massage, I had telephone conversations with potential clients. When they asked if they could pick their girl or said "full body massage" in a certain tone, I never allowed them to get close to my table. Email exchanges with potential overnight guests could be full of lies I might not uncover until it was too late. Truthfully, I could not imagine what they were going to lie about that would end up making their stay uncomfortable or awkward. I was nervous about this whole endeavor, having second thoughts about going through with it, and scared that if I changed my mind, I would not be able to pay the bills. I am sure it would have helped if I had been a guest prior to being a host, so I better grasped the nuances of this relationship. This surely would have instilled trust instead of the doubt and fear that consumed me.

A social media search of a potential guest was out of the question because until I hit the "approve" button I only knew the person's first name. I had to rely on my gut feelings so much at the get-go. Through the years Airbnb has improved its validation system for guests and hosts. It is possible to provide an array of identification, along with email and phone numbers to the company for it to verify who people are. Reviews are another source of information assuming both parties are honest. One host told me she would not tell the truth about less than desirable guests because she did not want to come across as being mean. I was shocked. I explained how hosts need to have each other's backs so we do not end up with a bad guest. My logic did not resonate with her. Clearly, there is no foolproof system to ensure guests are going to actually be people you would invite into your home even if money were not on the table. I had to trust that when people had nearly all good reviews, I was going to have a good experience. Mostly, this proved to be the case. After all, the guests were also taking a chance on me; that I represented my listing accurately and that the reviews were accurate. Guest reviews at the time had a five-star rating system for accuracy (meaning, did the description match the actual rental), check-in (how easy was it), cleanliness (people's expectations varied, like being surprised there was dog hair in the house and in their room when a dog lived on the premises), communication (how fast I responded to them as well as thoroughness of answering questions), location (this was completely subjective depending on what they liked to do and where they wanted to go), and value (another subjective category, but one I usually scored high in).

Celebrating a first anniversary led the initial couple to my Tahoe home. I was excited. Then I got a request for another booking. This was for the Saturday before Memorial Day weekend. Oh, geez, I was not ready. So much for having plenty of time to finalize the room. I spent what little spare time I had from my real job (that was more than full time) to ensure the Airbnb components were in place. A single guy was booking the room; a guy who had joined Airbnb that month so he had no reviews. So much for that being a method to screen him. It was obvious I was a single woman with a dog based on my profile. When listing the property online I was asked how many other people were in the house, as well as animals, so guests would know what they were getting into. I knew eventually I would have to decide about having a lone male in my house. I was not expecting to have to make that decision so soon. I could not figure out if my gut was trying to tell me to decline the request or if fantasizing about the cha-ching of money was more powerful, or if I was merely in unchartered waters that had me second guessing everything. As a massage therapist, when I had put money over instinct, it often was not a good outcome. I asked him to tell me a bit about himself. He worked in the Silicon Valley, had never been to Tahoe. His girlfriend messaged. They both were coming. *Phew*. Dilemma disappeared. I accepted them.

11

Nervousness and excitement filled me. How strange to realize strangers were going to be in my house. I repeatedly told myself to consider it a business transaction. It was money. It was better than a full-time roommate. Oh, the conversations I had with myself and AJ, the dog. At times it was like I had too many inner voices. All these *what ifs* went through my head, and they were not good scenarios. I stressed about random items in the house getting damaged or broken. Would the sheets be ruined? Would people be rude? Would it feel like my home? The fact there would be two of them with just me and a dog who was not all that protective concerned me. I wondered if I was doing the correct thing. I nearly talked myself out of the whole Airbnb gig and was ready to cancel the bookings. The positive was money. That money would help me keep the house, a house I really liked. Downsizing was not an option because of the housing market. Even becoming a renter was not logical. Early on I had looked at places to rent instead of buying out my ex, which is what led me to Airbnb. Rentals were crazy expensive and what was available was trashy for nearly the same amount as my mortgage payment. I had to make this work. I had to at least try it. The thought of a long-term roommate, someone always in my space who also could ruin my things helped reassure me this new venture was the correct choice. Belongings break, things need replacing, and there is no perfect person to live with even when it is romantic. I needed to calm down.

Initially the room cost $95 a night, of which I netted $92. Lodging taxes and cleaning fees are now the norm for most rentals but were not part of listing to start with. A load of laundry, a few extra lights on, the furnace chugging away when it normally would be off, and coffee were my basic additional expenses. I definitely came out ahead. The mortgage would partially get paid with every $92 increment. Airbnb'ers at this time were charged right when they booked. As a host I received my money the day after they checked in. Airbnb now keeps the money for several days before paying a host and often guests only pay half when they book, with the final payment due a couple weeks before arriving. While Airbnb takes a percentage from guests and hosts when a property is booked, there is no fee to have a listing or to browse places to stay.

The first guests emailed asking about a two- to three-hour hike. I suggested the Rubicon Trail starting at Emerald Bay on the South Shore of Lake Tahoe. I sent them a link to a story I had written about it. I never knew if they took my advice. It is a perfect trek in May, the month of their visit. So often in late spring it is hard to hike in Tahoe because several feet of snow in higher elevations make trails impassable without snowshoes. People coming from towns even a couple hours from Lake Tahoe have been in spring for months and forget or do not realize how snow can linger in the mountains long after winter is off their radar. Walking on the edge of Emerald Bay—one of the most photographed locations in the world—is stunning as the water's color goes through the spectrum of blues starting with turquoise and culminating with sapphire. Being mostly a flat single-track dirt trail, except for the mile up at the end on a paved road, it is an excursion people who are used to regular exercise can do even though the round trip is more than nine miles. I suggested this hike to many guests because it is easy to turn around midway and still have been immersed in incredible scenery. An added bonus is the offshoot along the trail near D.L. Bliss State Park to the Rubicon Point Lighthouse, which is one of the highest-elevation lighthouses in the United States. (The highest is in Frisco, Colorado.) Today, lighthouses are not a necessary navigational tool at Lake

Tahoe. However, in the early 1900s boats were one of the main methods of transportation in the Lake Tahoe Basin, so much so that Congress agreed to foot the bill for multiple lighthouses on the lake, each costing roughly $900 at the time. The Rubicon was one of four built in about 1919. A few years later it was decommissioned, with the one farther north along the West Shore at Sugar Pine Point State Park taking its place. For historical purposes the structure of the Rubicon lighthouse has been restored more than once this century because of vandalism. It still looks more like an outhouse than a traditional lighthouse. A battery-operated light at times is used for ceremonial purposes. To this day the Rubicon Trail is my favorite Lake Tahoe hike. For scenic quality this hike is rated nine out of a possible ten in my books *The Dirt Around Lake Tahoe: Must-Do Scenic Hikes* and *Lake Tahoe Trails For All Seasons: Must-Do Hiking and Snowshoe Treks*.

During the hiking guests' brief stay communication was nearly non-existent. Friends assured me this was a good thing because it increased the odds of not feeling like my space was being invaded. I paused to think about this. When I first contemplated doing this whole Airbnb thing, I fantasized about helping people enjoy the greater Lake Tahoe region. It would be like all the people who enriched my travels when I was backpacking through Europe in my twenties and when I traveled solo again in my thirties for four months in South America. So many locals had helped me discover special places in their hometowns, told me about attractions and points of interest to visit, regaled me with stories about the history of wherever I was, and directed me to restaurants that were never written about in any guidebook. I thought it would be fun to share travel stories with these strangers who would be in my home. I was in the last year of my forties, perhaps wanting to capture a part of that wanderlust through others. I was feeling a bit chained to Tahoe with owning and running a 24/7 online news site, not to mention being saddled with a mortgage payment. So much of me wanted to be a nomad. I fantasized that if I could live vicariously through my guests, it would satiate my desire to run away to some far-off land where work was no longer a necessity.

John and Denise, a super sweet couple, were my next guests. (Names of all guests have been changed.) English was not their primary language. As we were all leaving about the same time that first night, he pointed to his phone where it said T.J. Maxx was the town center. He asked if this is where they should go. I smiled, trying not to laugh. If they wanted to go clothes shopping or buy liquor at the neighboring BevMo!, that would be the place to go. I had never thought about where to send someone at night in Tahoe. I am more of a homebody in that I go out when there is an event, not just to go out. My outings mostly entailed meeting friends at a restaurant for dinner or going someplace for a drink. Guests wanted more than food and beverage ideas. Most did not want to stay in while on vacation. All the interesting things going on in Tahoe escaped me. In this case the language barrier prevented them from being able to express their interests in a way I could understand.

Finally, I suggested parking at any of the Stateline, Nevada, casinos. It would be a few years before each casino charged for parking so on this night it would be free. Once there, if they did not want to gamble, they could stroll around Heavenly Village on the California side to check out those shops and restaurants. Miniature golf is available in the summer months; then it turns into an ice rink in winter.

I mentioned the Hard Rock Hotel & Casino had recently opened. With its music memorabilia, it was more than slot machines and table games. The Stateline casinos do not have the razzle-dazzle of Las Vegas, but that is where the bulk of the entertainment on the South Shore can be found. It had been too many decades since I went clubbing to be able to offer advice in that arena. In my twenties I could stay out dancing until the wee hours of the morning and still usually make it to work. They were not dressed for the casino dancing scene, at least the little I knew about it. These two were much younger than me, on a mini vacation, expecting to do something fun with their time. I gave them credit for wanting to explore but wished I could have been more helpful. There is plenty to do on the South Shore of Tahoe—comedy, magic, music, movies. But to just wander, well, it is not like a big city where the hustle and bustle, interesting street characters, bright lights, and charm of individual neighborhoods are captivating without having to spend money. I never did get super proficient at nighttime ideas, but most people seemed to know about the casinos and would later tell me how much fun they had.

I do not know where these two ended up, but when I got back about 10 p.m. they were in their room. It was really my room. I was overcome by the sensation of feeling like I was a guest in my own home. This feeling never totally went away. How could it when I would always be heading to the guest room while guests slept in my room? This smaller room was comfortable, and I was used to it. I was there for five months before the other half of the twelve-year relationship moved out. Since then, I had reconfigured the furniture so the room looked and felt totally different. It was no longer claustrophobic, no longer penance for having been the one to end the relationship. Despite being an average size, the room could feel confining because I usually closed the door to give everyone more privacy. Looking out at the trees made it more pleasurable than the primary bedroom in terms of scenery. In the bigger room, the window behind the bed revealed the house next door, about six feet away. I needed to be happy in this new, smaller space for this Airbnb thing to work. I refused to let it feel like punishment. This was going to be the start to something fun and profitable, I told myself. Positive affirmations, I told myself.

## Adjusting to Shared Living

The closets in the house were so small it was impossible to share one with another person. My clothes had been in the guest room for years, so there was nothing to relocate when paid strangers were in the house. Only toiletries needed moving. It was not a big deal at first. I had been in the guest bath for five months as well, though I had moved back to the primary bedroom and bath when the house became all mine. As the bookings increased, hauling stuff back and forth got tiresome. I did not want to go into their space with or without their permission for fear of intruding. Plus, stuck in my head was the need to build up good reviews. I could only imagine what someone would write if they found me in their room even if my hands were filled with my toiletries. I would be understanding if I were in their shoes, but awfully skeptical at the same time. Having the bulk of my bathroom supplies in the guest bath made the most sense while being an Airbnb host. That way, my excuse not to floss disappeared, but I also no longer had to buy deodorant or something else because I forgot to move it before guests arrived.

From the get-go my goal was to go about my life as normally as possible when guests were in the house. This included keeping the thermostat set where I liked it. Fleetingly, I thought about putting a lock on the hallway gauge like so many offices have to curtail temperature wars. For me it would be about keeping the

17

utility bills in line with what I was accustomed to paying. I was also afraid karma was going to bite me in the wallet. After all, plenty of times I had jacked up the heat in hotels knowing I was not getting that electric or gas bill. I feared guests would do the same to me when I was out of the house. They had a right to expect to be comfortable temperature-wise. I was going to have to give a little on the heat to keep them happy. Cold guests might equal a frigid review. People almost always came from warmer climates, so what might feel fine to me could be uncomfortable to them. I only had to remember how my sister, who lived in a hot climate, could be cold at seventy degrees in Tahoe. She wore a sweatshirt when I was in shorts and short sleeves. Guests were going to be less than thrilled with how cool I liked it at night. Because I grew up in a house with the thermostat set at fifty-five degrees Fahrenheit overnight, I thought this was normal. This is the temperature I preferred most of my adult life as well. Things changed when I started living in the Tahoe house alone. I went into extreme frugal mode by turning the heat completely off. More than once I woke up able to see my breath. It was that cold inside. Various factors determine when condensation occurs, but forty-five degrees Fahrenheit or less is likely. That is a crazy inside temperature. It also meant it was even colder outside. The average low temperature in South Lake Tahoe ranges from twenty to forty-five degrees. Plenty of nights it was single digits outside, while a few times it went below zero. Cold air is great for sleeping as long as there are plenty of covers. Some studies say it is good for you. Citing these facts was not going to cut it with most guests, if any. Telling them the down comforter should be sufficient was also not likely to be met with a favorable response. I needed to be prepared to use some of my Airbnb proceeds to pay higher utility bills. I upped the thermostat to sixty degrees at night with paid guests sleeping in the house.

A hazard of an older house is it creaks like people do. Several early mornings a freight train-like noise rattled me out of a deep sleep. The electric meter was spinning, um, I mean the furnace started up because the inside temp had hit the sixty-degree mark. I rolled over hoping they did the same. Fortunately, no one complained about the loud heater. Once fully awake, I notched up the heat a bit. With the primary bedroom becoming like a sauna when the door was closed and heat was on, I did not want the furnace set too high. Seeing the primary bedroom window wide open one time while the heat was on taught me the hard way that the thermostat was too high. And to think my initial worry was about them being cold. Plenty of people sleep with windows partially open at night year-round. I could tell this was not what was going on. These people were hot. Paying to heat the outdoors was not something I could afford, nor did it make sense environmentally. Of course, I would have preferred the guests tell me they were roasting in the room. It was a fluke I saw the open window while going to my office. During most stays the bedroom door was closed whether people were in the room or elsewhere. This was one of those times it was to all of our benefit that I knew what was going on behind closed doors so I could make them comfortable in an economical manner.

I left about 9:40 the next morning while the strangers who left the window open were still behind closed doors. I heard them, but never saw them. Check out was at 11 a.m. I told them the night before it was no big deal to hang out longer. I did not know what it meant when they smiled but said nothing. They messaged asking to eat some of my cereal. Fine, I emailed back. I felt like I had no choice but to say yes. I did not care about the food; what I cared about was being accommodating so I would get that good review. By 11:30 a.m. they messaged to say they were gone. Maybe it was getting cold. I had turned the furnace off when I took off. They left a note in the guestbook saying they had a nice visit and that my dog was really friendly. No word about the temperature.

I washed the sheets and cleaned their room. The couple had cleaned the coffee pot, washed the mugs—even emptied the grounds. It was like they had never been there. Even so, I re-washed everything to ensure things really were washed with soap and water for the next people and not merely wiped clean.

During their brief stay I realized I am an exhibitionist. Typically, I would not shut the door when I was in the bathroom no matter the purpose of being there. This habit clearly had to change. Normally after showering I walked to my room to get clothes—again, naked. Even just a towel around me would be inappropriate if guests saw me for the brief time it took me to walk the four feet between the two thresholds. What if they startled me and I dropped the towel? What kind of review would that have elicited? I no longer owned a robe, so that was not an option for being more covered up. I brought a change of clothes in with me to the bathroom so I would be completely dressed when exiting the bathroom. Good thinking because going forward meeting people in the hallway leaving the bathroom was not unusual.

I was also known as the naked neighbor because of my penchant to hot tub in the nude. I had to dig through my newly arranged drawers to find my swimsuit to be "decent" when the room was booked. Plenty of times people returned while I was soaking, so being clothed was appropriate. I laugh reflecting on South Lake Tahoe City Council meetings where vacation home rentals were debated. Residents complained about having to see tourists next door or behind them in the buff using the hot tub. I cannot imagine the complaints they would have filed against me had I been their full-time neighbor. I am thankful my neighbors did not care about my clothing optional hot tubbing. I have no idea if guests were fully clothed. It was rare I popped my head out back to say anything while they were soaking. Usually, it was only to let AJ in and out. In the dark I could not tell who had what on.

After hot tubbing, I routinely walked around the house in a towel doing other stuff like getting a bite to eat, doing the dishes, watching television. This, too, had to stop when paid guests were around even with a swimsuit under the towel. These were not big adjustments, but they were not actions that came naturally. My regular exhibitionist behaviors returned when the room was not reserved.

## In Hot Water

I stayed in the guest room that next week because I did not want to change the sheets again. AJ the dog was content to sleep in the twin bed with me because she still had most of the mattress. I preferred the king bed even though with the dog sleeping horizontally I still had about the same space of a twin or possibly less.

Toni and Eric, the first couple to book a reservation, were coming for Memorial Day weekend to celebrate their first anniversary. Apparently, others are easier going than I am because celebrating any occasion with strangers in the house would not be high on my to-do list. I prefer privacy for milestones with a significant other. Lucky for my bank account plenty of other people are less fussy about such matters. It could have been all about money for them, that this type of lodging fit their budget. It might have been my room or no trip. Beyond economics, a private hot tub was a huge advantage to staying at my house compared to someplace else. Sharing one at a hotel means being with people who might be loud, splashing, peeing, or worse, there could be children. Most hotel spas are concrete and can be uncomfortable to sit in. Personal ones are usually fiberglass, which is softer on the skin. At my place they could control the temperature, as well as soak long past the normal 10 p.m. closing time at a hotel. I never knew if more than soaking took place. Ignorance brought me peace of mind.

When I started hosting no specific rules existed for owner-occupied rentals. On November 17, 2020, the South Lake Tahoe City Council finally adopted an ordinance strictly for these shared home rentals. The city limited "hosted rentals" permits to 200. Prior to the final passage I wrote a letter expressing my dissatisfaction with some of the proposals. Initially, the city wanted the host to be at the property when the guest checked in. That was absurd. I was rarely around when people showed up. This gave everyone more flexibility. There were nights when I was fast asleep as people retrieved the key out of the lock box and then found their room. I met them the next day. To have had to stay up, well, I am sure I would have made a grumpy first impression. Luckily, this requirement was dropped from the final ordinance. How the city would have enforced this rule is beyond me.

Another issue I had with the law as first written was that the host had to be within fifteen minutes of the rental at all times. I pointed out in my letter to the city that this would prevent many people from being able to go to work let alone go out for any length of time to enjoy Tahoe, or anywhere else for a day of fun. Even my dog walks were longer than a quarter hour. People drive more than fifteen minutes to shop because the basin has so few choices. Again, this requirement was scratched.

A final regulation I disagreed with was the inability to use the hot tub from 10 p.m. to 8 a.m. despite the rules matching what whole house rentals had to comply with. That time span was considered quiet hours. I have no idea what the city would do if a host invited her paying guests to use the hot tub during that time. After all, there were no rules prohibiting me, the homeowner, from soaking at any hour of the day or night. This rule took effect after I was out of the hosting business in South Lake Tahoe. When I had a listing, no limits existed about hot tub hours. Guests and residents could soak in hot water at any hour. The city has a noise ordinance so loud parties, early morning construction and other disturbances can be regulated. This is for everyone, not just people renting part or all of their house to tourists. Loud hot tubbing by anyone between 10 p.m. and 7 a.m. would fall under the noise ordinance. Therefore, a total ban of hot tubbing made no sense. My guests were conscientious about keeping their voices low, especially when the bubbles were going. Not once did I have to ask someone to be quiet. Even if I wanted to eavesdrop, everyone was too quiet for me to overhear what they were saying. None of my neighbors mentioned anything to me about loud guests. Plus, at most it was two people out there. I am sure the times I had several friends over we were louder than any of my paid guests. Even then, no complaints from the neighbors. It probably helped that I had talked to some of them ahead of time about my plans to become an Airbnb host.

Every morning after a guests' lengthy soak I would lift the hot tub cover knowing multiple chemicals would be needed to make the water look presentable and for me to know it was sanitary. Inevitably, the water was too murky to see the bottom, which was maybe three feet down at the most. This had to be more than body oils and lotions. So gross. Not once did I hear or see anyone come into the house to use the bathroom. Maybe they were watering the outdoor plants. After all, at times I found it more convenient to pee on the wood chips even though I did not have to walk as far as they had to for indoor plumbing. I would have been understanding if they relieved themselves in the yard. This would have been preferable to urinating in the hot tub. Most people were drinking a beverage while in the tub, adding to the probable need for a bathroom. I understood it could be super cold to get out, and even more of a pain to walk to the other end of the house since the actual guest bath was off limits to them because it was my private bathroom while they were there. Most guests took advantage of the solitude, staying in the hot tub for hours.

It was a given the hot tub got treated before and after every visit, but sometimes it was necessary to maintain it multiple times during stays. This was not something I expected to do based on how little upkeep was needed when I used the tub. Keeping it in pristine condition was a new job for me. It was something my ex took care of all the years we were together. It still amazes me I had to be talked into getting the hot tub. I had been a bath person all my life so one would think a permanent body of hot water would be a no brainer. Nope. At least not at first. However, once installed it was not long before I was using it the most. The price was right, too. The bulk of it I earned as a bonus through my job as the managing editor of what was the main newspaper in town at the time. The publisher traded advertising space for it. My ex had a prescription for it from her doctor because of her back so it was a tax write off for her. It was a sweet deal all around.

Before starting my Airbnb business, I had the hot tub company send out a couple workers to drain and clean the tub, then give me a primer on how to maintain it. I stocked up on chemicals that were not in the closet and invested in a few bottles of test strips so I would not just be throwing chemicals in without knowing if they were the correct ones. I was surprised by how much bromine I went through. It was good the test strips did not say what was in the water—pee, sweat, other bodily fluids, spilled wine, something unimaginable. The added maintenance was no big deal; after all I knew one of the selling points about the rental was the private hot tub. With the dark night sky at Tahoe, the stars dancing overhead could be stunning. This mesmerizing view was not something most people see at home, especially those coming from a metropolitan area. So much light pollution exists in most places. For those who know the constellations, it was easy to pick them out. I smiled when I would have to coax people into the tub while it snowed. This was when I loved that hot water the most. The silence of the snow falling, the whiteness of the landscape providing a unique natural light—it was magical. It was even better than on a full-moon night when that orb would become a spotlight, lighting up the yard and casting shadows otherwise unseen.

The house came with a small outside light that was almost useless. Decorative party lights illuminated about two-thirds of the back yard. Mostly I turned them on when dining out back or during parties. People shocked me when they wanted them on while in the hot tub. Artificial lights always ruined the mood for me—even with friends. It had nothing to do with romance. It was about appreciating Mother Nature. They had no interest in trying it without lights. Sometimes you cannot explain to people what they are missing, just like they were not going to be able to explain their light fetish to me. Maybe they were fearful of wild animals and did not want to admit it. To me, looking at all the stars, planets, occasional plane traffic and that rare shooting star were what made the hot tub such a relaxing attraction. It was all the entertainment I needed. On nights when sleep eluded me, the hot tub was often my refuge. In the wee hours of the morning the sky was even more dazzling because the number of stars had seemingly multiplied.

I learned the hard way not everyone likes a tub at one hundred and two degrees. As I was about to submerge my chilled body into that warm liquid I practically screamed. Then I panicked. Crap, I did not want to pay for a hot tub repair. The water, it was tepid, cold really. I looked at the setting. Ninety-eight degrees. What the heck? I got out. I was pissed—first, at my guests for not turning the temperature up when they got out and then at myself for not having checked it. Now I knew how they could stay in so long; it was not that hot. Unfortunately, it takes a hot tub longer to heat up than it does to cool down. I was slow to learn the temperature lesson because there were other times when I wanted a *hot* tub and ended up in a lukewarm tub or changing my plans.

One time, my friend, Brenda, and I were soaking when the Airbnb'ers returned. They were a young couple who did not know much about Tahoe. They joined us upon our invitation. This is the only time I recall hot tubbing with guests. I never thought about going in when people were already there, though there were plenty of times I was disappointed the tub was taken. A few times people invited me in, but I never knew if they were saying this to be polite since it was my hot tub after all, or if they were sincere. I always declined. If I really wanted hot water, I had a bath tub I could use. By the time the four of us got out we had polished off a bottle of wine, which I think was just between me and Brenda. It was one of those clear nights where the stars were bright, and snow covered the ground. Neither of us remember much about the man and woman who sat across from us. They did not say much as we regaled them with stories about life in Tahoe. They were most fascinated with tales of bear sightings and wondered if they would be lucky enough to see one. Not that visit, but other guests would see one of those majestic animals closer than they wanted to.

Specific hot tub towels were in the guests' room when they arrived. I asked that they not take them to the beach, but that policy was not always followed. Better that those towels be in the sand than the bath towels was how I rationalized this transgression. It would depend on the overall visit if I mentioned this house rule violation in the review. In the room were specific plastic glasses for any beverages consumed in the hot tub. The no-glass rule in the hot tub was one I had for myself and friends as well. It was a rule I enforced. It would be a nightmare to remove every shard of glass and would require draining the water. I did not want any down time with the hot tub for myself or others. I was usually in it twice a day, once as a midmorning break from pounding the keyboard for work and then before going to bed. The thought of the tub being off limits for a couple days to refill it and heat to one hundred two degrees was incentive to enforce the no-glass rule. Those who had a bottle of wine put it on the step or railing, then refilled glasses as needed. People who preferred drinking beer out of a bottle had to forego that habit while soaking.

## Uncomfortable at Home

When the Memorial Day weekend guests' arrival time was moved up, I knew I would not be at the house. AJ had never let strangers into her home before. Only people she knew had come in without me being there. No matter how much I talked to her about Toni and Eric coming, I was not convinced this was going to go well. At that time, she could be persnickety. I also knew there was no way I could be home for every arrival, and I certainly was not going to be around every hour guests were there. Nor could AJ go with me every time I left the house, whether it was for work or fun. Conversing in full paragraphs with her was the norm, so she was not fazed by the amount of talking. However, the urgency and tone in my voice were different. Finally, I was convinced she understood how important this was to me, and for both of us. Apparently, she was welcoming. They let her out back and in again. Now I wondered if I was even needed. Would she let anyone in or just people who knew her name? I soon learned to include on my welcome email to guests to act like they were AJ's best friend, and she would be theirs. This worked, until someone tried too hard.

When I finally arrived, I could smell something cooking in the kitchen. I could not pinpoint the aroma, but it was not meat. *Phew*. I had not told them to not cook or reheat meat or fish. A day before arriving, Toni asked about using the refrigerator and microwave because she had dietary issues. Being a vegetarian, I guess I could be classified as having dietary issues, too. I said, yes, those appliances were theirs to use. Whatever the food was in the microwave the smell did not linger too long. I had joined an Airbnb group for vegetarians and vegans. (They were not that helpful, so the fact they did not exist forever was no loss.) Those groups suggested allowing full kitchen privileges. One guy in some other country served a vegetarian breakfast. I was not about to feed my people. I did not even want them to feed themselves in any meaningful manner. I had one woman ask about breakfast, mentioning how B and B is part of the name. While Airbnb stands for AirBedandBreakfast, it is up to hosts what they provide for guests. The "air" in the business' name stems from the air mattresses the founders used when they launched the company. My listings never made it sound like food would be part of their experience. I explained to the hungry guest how all listings tell people what they can expect and apologized if she expected breakfast. This was one of many examples of how the person making the reservation did not share all the amenities with his guest. Other hosts offer food in the morning, even wine later in the day, which I have been the recipient of as a guest. I provided coffee in their room with sugar and creamer. If they needed more, they were on their own.

Eric and Toni, the anniversary celebrants, later headed off to the hot tub. They had a large bottle of cheap white wine in the fridge. I chose to open a nice bottle of Chardonnay to share with them. I took two glasses out to the hot tub and said this was a small gesture to help them celebrate. It really was about wanting them to have the best time possible, and not bribing them to get a good review. I was most surprised I was able to put my romantic woes aside and celebrate their marital bliss. I started a fire in the wood stove because it was getting cold in the house and the furnace was off. They were still soaking after I took AJ for a walk. (Their several-hour soak is what made me make the mental note to stalk up on hot tub chemicals.) After getting into dry clothes, they played cards in *my* living room while I ate dinner in the guest room, which was now my bedroom. My norm was to eat on the couch in front of the TV. Eating in my bedroom out of sight seemed less pathetic than sitting alone at the kitchen table. That I cared what it looked like was even more sad. AJ was not happy about being kept on my side of the door. She knew potato chips might be offered to her if she went to the living room. I had no human or canine treats in the bedroom for her.

After they went to bed about 7:45 p.m., I opened the door to feel less confined. I had work to do and chose to do it from the bedroom and not the office. All was quiet except for the blower on the wood stove. Then I heard strange noises. I listened harder

29

to make sure I was hearing what I thought I was hearing. Yep, my sheets were soiled. At least someone in the house was having sex. This was not going to be the last time this happened. It was just not something I had thought about in advance—what all might happen in my room, on my bed. Sleeping on hotels beds where other people had sexual interludes never crossed my mind, nor did I consider what happened on the beds of friends and family members before I visited. I never thought about what people did on my guest room bed. Suddenly, other people's sex lives mattered. It was not jealousy, but instead disgust with what was happening on my bed. It was personal. I did not want to look at guests differently the next morning or say something like: "How could you on my sheets, in my bed?" Or even "good for you two!" I was not about to add "no sex" to the house rules. Imagine trying to enforce it. I deliberately told myself to stop thinking about what went on behind closed doors on any bed.

It was time for guests to have their own sheets and towels. No more sharing. It did not matter how hot the water was in the washing machine I could not wash away images in my head of my soiled linens. I needed something to be mine. Sharing everything was not going to happen anymore. It surprised me I did not think about this before I became a host. My mom convinced me that at a minimum I should have flannel sheets in winter for the guests, especially with wanting to keep the thermostat so low. She had already converted me to being a fleece sheet lover, though I had to experience them both to be convinced there is a huge difference in warmth between fleece and flannel. Fleece with two people can be too warm, so flannel is what guests would sleep on. They ended up having their own summer and winter sheets, as did I. Guest towels were in the primary bath, while my towels were in the guest bath. It worked and no longer was I grossed out, except for the sounds and finding evidence of safe sex.

When I got home the next day the fornicating guests told me they had locked themselves out of the bedroom. I was perplexed. How was that possible? In the twelve years I had lived in this house I never realized there was a lock on the primary bedroom door. I learned later my ex had no idea either. The lock did not want to be picked and getting something into the door jamb to pop it open was not working. My handyman neighbor was gone for the long weekend. The window was shut, so no attempting entry that way. Neither of the guests was any help so I was going to have to figure this out on my own as they stood there watching.

I took a hammer to the hollow door. No joke. It worked. Door was open. I could have used the chain saw to really show them mountain woman skills but figured that would be overkill and perhaps a bit alarming. Had this cheap wood been suitable for the stove I might have gone that route. I would have tried harder to find a less dramatic way to enter the room had I not been planning to replace those interior doors that summer. I have no idea what that option might have been. Kicking in the door was bound to cause damage to the door jamb and might have made closing the door impossible. A locksmith on a holiday weekend was not going to be cheap. I wondered if Airbnb would have refunded me the expense or if I could have gotten the guests to pay for it. The latter I figured was a no-go. While it was their fault the door was locked, they did not know any better. It is a reasonable assumption there would be a key to go with any lock, even if they did not have it in their possession.

Early on I did not require a deposit. No good explanation why not. Maybe I thought it would be a turnoff to potential guests or maybe I was too trusting or naïve about habits. On the Mexico house I instituted a $1,500 deposit from the start. I never needed to test how easy or difficult it is to convince Airbnb to pay out on a deposit or if the process to request reimbursement is simple or cumbersome. All I knew was, there was a limited amount of time to file a form requesting some or all of the deposit.

This lock incident taught me to include in my welcome email a blurb about not locking the bedroom door except if they wanted to while they were in the room. In most places in the world locking doors is about safety for us and security for our belongings. However, locking the door is not likely to keep any owner or host out of a room. It is like hotels having a universal key; private homeowners are going to have one as well. Assume a host has a key to every lock—at least every lock she knows about.

While all of this was going on, I got another booking. This one was for July 10-12 from a guy and his girlfriend from Paris. They would be going to San Francisco, Tahoe, Yosemite, and Monterey—some of California's most iconic locations. I was really looking forward to them, as they would be my first international travelers. I fantasized about them being more interesting to talk to than people from the San Francisco area. I lived too many years in the Bay Area to be interested in hearing stories about it. The Parisians would probably need my tour guide services more. We could talk travel and world adventures.

Then Karen from Florida sent a request for her brother and his wife to stay a Sunday-Tuesday. That seemed odd, especially when she had no reviews. Why was he not booking his own room? Because she was paying for it, she said. They were coming to scatter her husband's ashes at Lily Lake in Desolation Wilderness, which was not too far from my house. She told me I could find out more about her on Facebook. Not much there based on her settings, so that was not a useful suggestion. I learned she was in her seventies. She planned to stay in a condo at a resort on the Nevada side with relatives, but said if I would prefer, she would stay with me instead of her brother. I told her I was fine with her brother. Having buried my dad's ashes four years earlier, a year after he died, I knew this could be a hard time.

The brother and his wife arrived later than planned, which I learned was going to become the norm with guests. It takes longer to get to Tahoe than what people allow time for. Such are the hazards of driving windy mountain roads no matter from what direction one comes. I should have known things were not going to go well when they saw AJ go out the front door and they still shut it. Knowing she would not go far I showed them to their room. I explained the hole in the door. I did not want them to think there had been a fight or anything untoward. It was a weird conversation. I lied by telling them new doors were on order. I did not anticipate how strange it would be to have guests stay with a hole in the door. By the time the next paid visitors arrived the hole was covered, which made a world of difference. Eventually, new interior doors for the whole house were installed, but this was well after many guests had stayed behind the damaged door.

Later that night the couple involved with the ash scattering returned to the house while I was talking to my ex in her truck. She was furious at me for something I had posted on social media. She had given me a lift to a party at mutual friends', which I should have declined. This all added to the weirdness of the night. We ended our conversation quickly so I could beat the guests inside in case they let the dog wander outside again. For all I knew they would think my being out front in a vehicle was reason to let AJ out front. Truthfully, I just wanted to go to sleep and put this day behind me.

The duo came inside as I was letting AJ in from the back yard. I asked how dinner was. He said OK in a voice that sounded untruthful. Then he said something like "We have problems." I asked if there was anything I could do. He said no. I chalked this up to the stress of family and the reason they were all gathered. I went about my business of getting ready for bed. A commotion outside the bathroom had me speed things up. Suitcases were rolling down the hall because they were leaving. He said others in their group were not comfortable with them staying at my place, so they were going to the condo across town. I was at a loss for words, and conflicted. Why was he silent when I asked minutes ago if things were fine? Did he think he could leave unnoticed while I was in the bathroom? I did not like them, but still felt hurt my house was not what they wanted. He broke the short silence by saying it was complicated. Family and death always are. Family should be together at a time like this. One group at my house and one elsewhere did not make sense. They were too far apart. The widow would have known the distance between the rentals from previously owning a house near mine. Grief, though, seldom has anyone functioning at a high level, let alone logically.

The man handed me the key without looking me in the eye. I bet he did not have a say in leaving. His wife seemed like a piece of work. It all felt so weird. I was unnerved. A strange, unsettledness took over the house. Something felt off, like there was more going on than they were saying. Their uneasiness had me feeling uneasy. Something was being left unsaid that I felt like I should know, but they were not sharing. I checked the room. Nothing missing or damaged, but it seemed weird the shower door was open. The hand towel went into the dirty laundry basket, then I put things like the coffee and creamer back in their places when guests were not in the house. I longed for sage to cleanse the air. So much for getting to bed right away, let alone being able to sleep.

I wondered if I would get paid since they did not stay a full night. The humanitarian in me said I should refund their money.

The businesswoman in me said no way. They had not canceled via Airbnb, which prevented me from renting the room to others for that night and the next ones. Crap. This was so not how I envisioned this whole Airbnb thing working. They left me feeling uncomfortable in my own home. I could not put my finger on it. I did not want to be alone. I was not scared, just uneasy. While I had the key from the lockbox, I wondered if they would come back. After all, they had the place booked and would have a right to return. I did not know if I could prevent them from entering if they changed their minds again. I always wondered if people would make a copy of the key and come back later to harm me or the place. Those were unnecessary fears, but the imagination can be powerful. I broke down and texted my ex, asking her if she wanted to spend the night. Apparently, it was going to be a night of drama.

The drama, though, did not end that night. A few days later Karen, the woman who booked the room for her disappearing relatives, called. She said the couple left because they did not feel comfortable with the hole in the bedroom door. What the hell, I thought. I asked if she knew why there was a hole and how little it was? I could tell my version of the truth was much different from what her brother and his wife told her. Her sister-in-law told her the bathroom was not clean. Maybe the shower door was open because she was inspecting it for cleanliness. I told her it had been professionally cleaned. True, but that was two months ago. I had, though, kept it pristine going forward. Karen explained how her relatives were used to a higher-end place, that they like staying at her house, and at bed and breakfasts. My head was swirling. The room was in a fifty-year-old house, with pictures on the listing to prove it. Nothing about the photos made any aspect of the house look better than it was. These were not high-end glitzy real estate photos. Breakfast was never mentioned anywhere. If that was what was desired, stay where it is provided. It made me wonder what Karen had told her relatives about my place. Had she oversold it? The more this woman talked, the more I was hurt and pissed. She was insulting my home. It took all my restraint not to swear at her, not to hang up on her, not to tell her where she and her sister-in-law could go.

I was aghast when she told me she had left me a review. How was this even possible when she had never stepped inside my house? I was not going to review her because I had never met her. I was worried whatever she wrote would harm future bookings. Based on how she verbally trashed my home, I was fearful of what the review would say. It would undoubtedly be horrible, but worse it would be a lie being written by someone who had never set foot inside or outside of the property. Later she texted to say she tried to revise the review, but an Airbnb employee did not think it was bad enough to let her change it. I promptly emailed Airbnb my side of the story. They took a while to get back to me. Both parties have two weeks to write a review after the date of checkout. Once this happens the reviews are visible online. If only one writes a review, it is on the site after the fourteen-day period. Airbnb explained how they frown on third-party bookings, that it goes against their whole business philosophy. They did not have to explain it to me. This experience taught me the lesson to never accept a booking from someone who would not actually be staying in my home. Karen texted to say Airbnb employees changed their minds about publishing her review. I wonder what else they had to say to her. Her review never saw the light of day, so I do not know what it said.

CHAPTER TWO
# Interacting with Strangers

## Wildlife Encounter

Out of breath, the guests came running into the house barely able to spit out the words that a bear was in the garage. "Really? How cool," I said to them. I never got tired of seeing these creatures. They are magical beings. In Lake Tahoe it is black bears that call the area home. Their actual coloring can be lighter—brown, cinnamon, even blonde. They are not aggressive unless someone gets between a momma and her cubs or an individual does something else that would fall into the stupid category, like getting too close for a selfie or trying to touch the animal. I ran outside with my camera. This does not fall into the stupid category because of the distance I kept. One can never have enough bear photos was my mantra. I turned around when I heard the front door shut, thinking the guests came back out, but no one was there. Apparently, they felt more secure with walls separating them from the bruin.

Once back inside I asked if they had gotten any pictures. An adamant, "No." Their eyes seemed as big as the bear's paws and they may have been literally shaking. They looked at me as though I was a lunatic for going outside where wild animals roamed, and that I must be completely mad for staying there until I got all the pictures I wanted. Like I said, I was not that close. You never want to get too close because this is a wild animal. With one swipe of its paw, a person can be seriously injured or worse. Running is the last thing you should do when you encounter a bear. They can easily outrun anyone—even Usain Bolt, the fastest man alive. Black bears have been clocked at more than thirty-five miles per hour, while the famous sprinter has hit twenty-seven miles per hour. This would not be the only time I shared bear photos with guests. Less fearful humans sent me photos, expressing how witnessing these wild animals in their natural habitat was the highlight of their trip. Guests saw bears in the neighborhood, while hiking, and being out and about in town.

Anxiety eased for the fearful guests after learning how these animals are out looking for food and that humans are not on the menu. Unfortunately, though, human food has become a staple in the diets of too many bears. They have become known as garbage bears because they rummage through people's trash cans, get into vehicles, and on occasion break into houses. Even with all the educational campaigns throughout the greater Lake Tahoe area, plenty of people still put their garbage cans out the night before trash day. The trash company on the South Shore of Lake Tahoe tried to thwart this behavior by changing pick up times to not start before 7 a.m. Even that did not change everyone's habits. It is one thing for tourists to be unknowing, but when locals have total disregard for the wildlife, they should be reprimanded. Leaving garbage out hours before it is scheduled to be hauled away should be a criminal offense. After all, the animals were living in the forest long before humans started paving it over. Too many people did not care, though. Instead, they had the attitude that human convenience should trump wildlife. While these people were in the minority, their behavior could be fatal for bears. The mantra is "a fed bear is a dead bear." In other words, bears that get used to eating human garbage become a "nuisance" bear and can be killed by state wildlife officials. I did not understand why bear boxes were not mandatory throughout the Lake Tahoe Basin, or in all mountain communities. These locked metal containers usually hold two regular trash cans, though larger ones that accommodate bigger households, or vacation rentals are available. These bear-proof containers also allow people to put out their trash when they want without being detrimental to wildlife. After all, it is not just bears foraging for food—so do raccoons, coyotes, birds, and dogs. For an area that professed to be environmentally friendly, Tahoe tended to have policies that proved otherwise.

Besides not being good for their normal diet, when bears get used to eating human food, they keep looking for it. It is easier than scrounging for berries or fish or other healthy foods. It was the dog food in the garage that had lured this particular bear to my place. While AJ unwittingly shared some of her kibble, nothing else was disturbed. Once these bears get a taste for human (or dog) food they can become more aggressive in their desire to continue this diet. A bear that breaks into a house is likely to wind up having to be killed. People can be granted a depredation permit, meaning they can trap the animal and then have it killed by state regulators. California and Nevada, the two states that split Lake Tahoe, differ on how they handle nuisance bears and reckless people. Social media has never been kind to those who want to do harm to a bear whether it was intentional or otherwise.

I cleaned up the mess, put the garage door down, and the excitement was over. No bears ever tried to break into the garage. Maybe the kibble was not that good. To ease the guests' shock about seeing this animal that weighed more than both of them combined and was bigger around than probably all three of us tied together, I went into a little more detail about the tranquil nature of black bears, how they are not killers unless provoked. It was after this encounter I realized I needed to tell guests to bring all food inside. Even a container of oil for a vehicle can look like a food carton to a bear. They can open car doors. They even know what coolers look like and that they contain tasty morsels. These are not dumb animals. I did not share with guests that bears can open house doors, too. No reason to scare them unnecessarily. I wanted them to enjoy themselves, not think they were in some wild animal kingdom.

While these guests were aware this was a wild animal, there are plenty of tourists who forget that fact or do not seem to appreciate it. Not far from the Tahoe house is an area where, in the fall, bears like to feast on the salmon swimming upstream in the creek to spawn. It is an annual ritual for these fish to come from Lake Tahoe up Trout Creek to where they had been born. For bears, it is like a buffet. With how shallow the water is in the fall, it can also be easy pickings for the unsuspecting Kokanee salmon. While they were going to die naturally after spawning, some had a more rapid demise. Tourists could not get enough of this cycle of life in the wild. In their desire to take a selfie with a bear, they were encroaching on the animals' habitat. What would you do if someone were practically in your lap as you ate? Probably say something, even push back a bit. Well, when a bear does this, it is considered aggressive; it is the one to blame, not the people. It will be the bear that is put down, not the person banned from coming back or cited or even fined. To prevent a deadly encounter, the U.S. Forest Service created a walkway farther away from the wildlife because people could not figure out their behavior was potentially confrontational. It is too bad common sense could not prevail. Now everyone is a greater distance from the action all because of a few careless, selfish people. To further prevent bear-human encounters, federal officials finally prohibited people from certain areas while bears seek out the Kokanee salmon. People are slow learners so more rules must be enacted to prohibit the rest of us from enjoying Mother Nature's show. One day, people will probably be banned from this part of Tahoe during the entire spawning season to spare the bears. If that is what it takes to ensure the bears survive, so be it.

## Simple Pleasures

A flash of light caught my eye as the two young women opened the door. At first, I panicked thinking the room was aglow with candles. "No candles" was one of those rules I added after the fact. Allowing them seemed like a fire waiting to happen. Who would be liable? Me because I never said no to them? The guests because they are the ones who struck the match? Would this fall under Airbnb's insurance policy? I never wanted to find out the answers to those questions. I had a significant other who liked to travel with candles that required a match, so I understood the allure to create a certain ambiance. Until becoming an Airbnb host, I never thought about any potential danger or the threat of wax ruining carpet when I traveled. Wax candles are not something I travel with today, nor would I ever again for the very reasons I did not want them used by guests. Luckily, not too many people could have "legally" used candles before I saw guests with them.

Not wanting to be confrontational, I let those burn. I rationalized I was in the house if anything horrible happened. Not the best logic, but I was still establishing boundaries and figuring out how to get what I wanted without being overbearing. I never caught anyone with candles after the rule was in place. "No candles" got added to the house rules that also included no drugs, parties, or people who were not staying at the house. The latter meant guests could not have friends over. In addition to the fire hazard, I did not want candle wax spilling all over because it is hard to get wax out of a carpet, especially from a red candle. Even the blow dryer trick did not work on one spot at the Tahoe house. Fortunately, it was not in a location most people would see.

In retrospect, I wish I would have put a few battery-operated candles in the room. Who knows if that would have been creepy or considerate in my attempt to set the mood for couples. Clearly, it would be optional if they wanted that setting. Why I would want to encourage intimacy is beyond me since I hated hearing sex sounds and picking up condom wrappers. With the Tahoe place being just a room, and often couples who rented it, it was a bit of a romantic getaway for folks. People came to celebrate anniversaries, birthdays, holidays, and to reconnect. Whereas the Mexico house was a true vacation spot that did not necessarily have anything to do with an event other than getting away from home.

The Mexico house came with a candle in a kitchen drawer that I left in case the electricity went out. Power would go out for no apparent reason, though it usually did not last long. Such are the realities of being in a Third World country. Again, why I did not supply battery operated candles for that house makes me wonder what I was thinking. One group in Mexico bought a few citronella candles for the outside patio to ward off mosquitoes. At worst, if they got knocked over, they would shatter on the concrete with nothing to burn. I assumed they were not taking them inside because of the unpleasant smell. Not knowing how responsible the next guests might be, I took those candles upstairs after they departed. For blackouts, flashlights were in each bedroom of both rentals. It was not unusual in Tahoe for the lights to go out in storms, especially if a tree full of snow fell onto a utility line.

As for that light that caught my eye, I took a second glimpse into the room to see what the glow was. Ah, it was Christmas decorations. The two women let me take a closer look. Wow! The exterior of the dresser was encased with a string of colorful lights, covering each drawer and the knobs. It provided just enough illumination to fill the room, so no other light was needed. This festive setting restored my belief, even if just momentarily, that there can be joy in the holidays.

These two had had a rough few weeks. One of their sisters had died unexpectedly. Had I lost one of my three sisters at their age, it would have been heartbreaking. I struggled to find profound words of comfort, but words of any kind were not going to help in this situation. The love these two young women had for each other was touching. I wanted to do whatever I could to make their time at my place even more special. Giving them space, letting them be themselves, sharing in their grief and their celebration of the season were what I could offer. Their affection and warmth toward one another were gifts to me. I regret not telling them how their joy even in their time of pain filled me with gratitude. Perhaps they saw it in my smile and the tenderness I tried to convey.

# Intimate Entanglements

Before the first Airbnb'er booked, friends wondered if I would hook up with a guest or two or maybe more. After all, I was single and being a host would be one way to meet new people. No commitment. No heartache. And no doubt it would put an exclamation point on sleeping with strangers. Friends assured me it would be fun to get back in that saddle. More than one gave me condoms, assuming I would be returning to my original team when it came time to choose a significant other or just a one-night stand. After being a host for a bit, another friend sent me an article about hookups made between Airbnb guests and hosts and wanted to know if I could have been quoted for the article. "No, not yet," I disappointed her.

Airbnb presumably does not have a statistic for the number of intimate encounters that happen between guests and hosts. Marketing and legal executives would have a field day if that data were collected. It would be enlightening to know if these brief interludes affected a review for the positive or negative. Oh, the detail and honesty that could be out there for the world to read if one chose to write a review about their sexual Airbnb experience. I wonder if much editing is done by Airbnb on reviews when it comes to colorful language and raunchy descriptions. Some long-term relationships must have started with an overnight stay. Social media and news sites reveal hookups between guests and hosts are definitely happening.

I had no desire to go down that road. I imagined it would only complicate things. For so many reasons my reaction was: Why bother? How do you keep living with someone for the length of his (or her) stay when you need to get on with your life? They have paid to be there, so I could not ask them to leave. What if I wanted to play around another night and they said no? That would be awkward in my home, just as it would be uncomfortable if I turned them down for another go round.

On occasion a guest turned my head, but not to the point of anything more than they were nice to look at. Only one guest seemed to have wanted more. Even after way too many margaritas I had my senses about me to make it upstairs alone. He was a guy from the United States who had a place on the other side of Baja California Sur known as the East Cape. This sixty-year-old was hoping to have some real bonding time surfing with his twenty-two-year-old son who was in college. The kid, though, was in his first serious relationship and was more interested in showing his girlfriend the sites of Baja than having father-son time, at least for the entire visit. This was the first time dad had to share his son and he was less than thrilled the dynamics had changed. He was having a hard time giving them space, treating them like adults, and accepting his boy was now a man with interests beyond father-son adventures.

Dad mentioned sharing a margarita later. Sure, why not, I thought. I had shared cocktails with other guests. When they got back from the water, he messaged asking if I was still interested in a drink, adding he could bring them upstairs. With it raining, that would have meant drinking inside my room. No way. AJ did not like other people in our room I told him, even though I am sure she would have let just about anyone in. I was more discriminating, especially with the bed being the most comfortable and prominent place to sit. Neither of us was going to start there. Even if I thought I might want more than a drink, no interlude with a stranger was going to start in my bedroom.

We imbibed downstairs under the covered patio. The young couple did not join us because they thought it a little weird to be fraternizing with the host. That made three of us because I could tell dad had intentions beyond sharing one of his fantastic margaritas. Had I picked up on the vibe earlier I would have said no to the drink so as not to mislead him. He was not kidding about his ability to make a mean margarita. Too delicious because I know I had at least three. This was on an empty stomach. I am sure he told me how he made them, but I was not able to retain the information being under the influence. I had no food to bring to the table to share. He had a few tortilla chips. That absorbed some of the alcohol, but most went to my head.

In the hours we talked he shared most of his life story, much of which I do not remember. The booze did not allow me to absorb the conversation. What I shared is a blur as well. His marriage was falling apart; his wife was back in the United States. The still married part was reason enough to do nothing more than drink with him. If I wanted a one- or multi-night stand, that would be one thing, but to play a part in the dissolution of a relationship really was not something I wanted to be part of at this stage in my life. I learned about his health issues, that he had a colostomy. He went on to share how he developed special clothing for people like himself, so it was not obvious. "Too much information!"—I wanted to scream. Apparently, my facial expression did not convey what I was thinking because he kept yacking away. While he was proud of what he was doing and not self-conscious about his bouts with cancer, he smelled. His bag had to be full. The stench was so off-putting I put my hands to my face to help diffuse the aroma. It was more offensive than any other body odor. It even lingered after he checked out.

Despite wanting to gag at times, I kept talking to this dude because I was starved for human interaction. Being new to Todos Santos meant friendships had not developed yet. No one to call to go for a drink, walk dogs with, or just hang out with. That is why a night of talking to someone other than my dog was so refreshing. Even getting a bit tipsy was fun because that was not happening on my own either. Still, all I was craving was chatting, nothing more. We went to our respective rooms alone without it being awkward.

When it came time to clean after the trio left, I found the dad's iPad buried in the bedding. I knew it was his because I knew who had slept in which room. I wondered if the device was left behind on purpose to necessitate a repeat visit. Dread filled me just thinking about it. While he was a decent guy, nice enough looking, seemed smart, and athletic, there was zero chemistry. I hoped an evening of cocktails had not misled him in any way. Not remembering what all I said that night was coming back to haunt me. Did I say something to encourage him there could be more another time? Was an overactive imagination getting the better of me? What if he really left the device behind by accident? Several weeks later with his cousin and her husband in tow he was in Todos Santos to retrieve his iPad. They were too chatty, and too interested in me and the house. I was being checked out. The couple talked about wanting to buy in Baja, maybe on my side of the peninsula. They mentioned potentially renting the house via Airbnb. I was as polite as I was standoffish. Now there was no way anyone could misinterpret my intentions. I wanted nothing to do with him. As a guest, he was great. I gave him a wonderful review and received one in return. Both were appropriate. Much to my relief I never heard from him again, nor did his relatives ever book the house.

For the record, as a host I always slept in my bed and only with my dog.

# Big Waves

Before my leaving the United States for Mexico several people mentioned what a great surfing location Baja California Sur is, especially the area where I would be staying. So, it came as no surprise I had a number of guests who traveled to Todos Santos for the waves. More than one father-son duo came for that purpose. I was not sure the two who booked for ten nights were going to have a great trip because their first night was fitful after the smoke alarm/carbon dioxide detector went off at 1 a.m. I was oblivious to this disturbance because they did not message me until hours after it first started its repetitive beeping. That obnoxious noise did not penetrate the concrete construction of the house, so I never heard it. I wonder if I would have gone downstairs to turn it off or tried to wake them up if I had. More likely I would have laid in bed, tossing and turning while I got more irritated with them for not doing anything about it and wondering how they could be sleeping through that noise. Unbeknownst to me they were getting perturbed with me as I slept soundly.

When I finally looked at my phone after playing tennis and going out for breakfast, there was a text message, voicemail, and another message through Airbnb from the dad. All were after 11 a.m. The dude was complaining about a high-pitched sound that had been going off for the last ten hours. He wrote, "Makes sleeping impossible!" I am sure it did. I have no idea why they endured the noise that long. Crazy, even stupid, I thought. I cannot believe they did not try to contact me sooner. I was upstairs most of those hours. They could have knocked on my door in the middle of the night if I did not respond electronically. And who does not know what a smoke alarm going off sounds like when the battery is dead or dying? I would never have let it wail all night. I would have hunted it down until I could silence it. They knew the sound was coming from the living room but could not find it. The device was sitting out on a shelf in a prominent location. It was not on the ceiling because the house is made of cinder block, and any hole becomes rather permanent. Plus, with no ladder, it would have been impossible for guests to reach the ceiling to take out the battery to stop the noise in a situation like this. I had no way of reaching the ceiling either.

The sixteen-year-old son finally figured out it was the smoke/carbon dioxide device, which they let me know at 11:22 a.m. I did not get an apology off to them until 12:27 p.m., when I received all the messages. I offered to put in a new battery, take it away, whatever they wanted. Dad said they dismantled it and all was good. For all I knew they had used a hammer to kill the sleep-depriving noisemaker.

When I met them in person later that day, I was humble and overly apologetic. It would not be the only time acting was required as a host. Part of it was sincere, part of it was to solicit a good review. I felt bad, but still wondered how they could be that blind to not find the alarm sooner. I wondered if the lack of review on their part had to do with the smoke alarm incident, something else or if he was one of those guests who never leaves a review. No review is certainly better than a bad review. I would have hated to receive demerit points for something that was out of my control and that I was never given a chance to rectify in a timely manner. Perhaps male pride or embarrassment allowed them to endure the obnoxious chirping instead of immediately asking for help especially from a woman. I appreciated the consideration to not wake me, but they would have had every right to and really should have.

In person the dad was in a much better mood compared to when he sent me the texts, saying it was all good and these things happen. A great day of surfing assuredly helped with the attitude adjustment. Their tales of the water proved they were having a fantastic time. Excitement filled their voices talking about even better waves being in the forecast for the week. Until moving to Todos Santos, I never knew a surf forecast existed. Information includes water and air temperatures, wave height, high and low tides, wind direction throughout the day, and sometimes a webcam to see what is going on in real time at a specific beach. Knowing this information was available before I took surfing lessons would not have helped. It is like a foreign language, so the significance of the numbers is lost on me.

Cerritos Beach, just south of Todos Santos, is where dad and son with the alarm issue spent their first two days. It is one of the most approachable places in the Todos Santos area for surfers, as well as being a sought-after location for swimmers and boogie boarders. It is also where beginners go to learn. People throughout the world come to this spot twenty minutes south of Todos Santos solely for the wave action. It is a growing community steps from the water. Commercial development on the sand in Todos Santos proper is met with social media chastising and lawsuits, while some predict Cerritos will be a mini-Cabo San Lucas one day with big hotels dotting the landscape.

The sandy bottom is a plus for those wading into the water without any kind of board. The riptide is less intense compared to most beaches along this stretch of the Pacific Ocean. On the third day of surfing this duo from Southern California opted to take the day off. The waves were going to be too big for them. Big waves even without a storm are why people travel to this stretch of Baja. Every day on my dog walk at the beach in Todos Santos the ocean would look different. Sometimes the swell was nothing, almost like it was a calm lake. Other days there would be no way I would venture out even if this were a swimmable beach. It was good the

50

dad was not pushing it, that he was being responsible by knowing their ability levels. Plus, there is so much to do in the region besides surfing.

I figured with living at the ocean I should learn how to surf. It would be like calling Lake Tahoe home and never taking a skiing or snowboarding lesson. Inevitably a lost opportunity to try something new and embrace what the local community has to offer. It is not like you can surf or ski just any place. One of the most reputable surf schools at Cerritos Beach offered five, two-hour lessons. Everyone I asked recommended the same school. Enough U.S. dollars were on me to cover all the lessons in case payment in full was expected upfront. The expense was a birthday gift to myself. The owner of the school communicated via email in decent English, which was encouraging. Of course, he could have been using Google Translate or some other app, which is what I relied on to communicate in Spanish. Even though the owner said he or another guy would meet me that first morning, no one was at the location at the appointed time. A handful of employees arrived about twenty minutes later. I had not yet learned that punctuality in Mexico means something different than what I was used to. I should not have been fazed since I came from a place where it was called "Tahoe time" because hardly anything started on time there. In Mexico it was even worse at least in terms of when people might show up for an appointment, not necessarily a large group meeting as was the case in Tahoe. I sat in a chair close to the water as I was told to do. Waiting in Mexico, I learned, is normal.

I never met Mario or the other guy he talked about, but Sergio was a likable enough instructor. It would have helped if one of us knew more of the other's native language. I will be the first to admit I should be able to speak the language of the country I am living in beyond being able to order beer and wine and asking where the bathroom is. At the same time, because the surf school caters to tourists and wants to be paid in U.S. dollars, they should speak English. At least that was my belief. Clearly, it was not theirs. Sergio demonstrated on land how to paddle, stand up, turn, and presumably surf with my arms stretched perpendicular to the board for balance. Being proficient on land after a few tries, we were quickly off to the warm water. Sergio never asked what my comfort level was in the ocean, how well I could swim, or anything about me. This seemed alarming for such a dangerous sport. My fingers were crossed that my towel, T-shirt, flip flops, car keys, and wad of cash left on the beach by my assigned chair would be there when I returned. My gut said not to tell anyone affiliated with the surf school about the valuables left behind even though it did not appear anyone was keeping an eye on my things. This scenario was likely repeated every day, multiple times a day without negative consequences.

After an hour went by, Sergio conveyed the surf was rough and that it would be better to finish the other hour of the lesson when the tide was lower and waves smaller. It would have been like learning to snow ski on moguls in a blizzard, or so I told myself as I justified quitting early. My neck was sore from the waves smacking me in the face as we paddled out. My right knee was bruised from all the times Sergio lifted my legs to put them together as we headed out. I had no idea if my legs needed to be together for some technical reason or if this made it easier for him to see around me or for some other reason he did not share. I left wondering why the school would take a beginner out in those conditions, and I was not the only rookie that day. Sure, they need to make a buck, but the surf school owner knew I lived locally and could presumably come any day, any time. Why not schedule this when it would be a more pleasant experience? With social media being a tool for businesses and consumers throughout the world, this surf school should be more cognizant of guest relations. Leaving reviews other than for Airbnb guests is not something I regularly do, and a negative one was not how I wanted to start my stay in Baja. The good part was no one asked for money. I figured settling up would occur when I finished the first lesson. I messaged the owner, told him what happened and said I would come again. Unfortunately, the pain in my neck and leg lingered for days, with ice required on the knee to bring down the swelling. I had second thoughts about how necessary it was to learn the local sport, especially when I was playing in a tennis tournament the next month. That was my priority, so staying healthy and uninjured were paramount. When the day arrived for lesson number two I emailed the owner, lying about why I would not be showing up. I never tried to surf again, which I regret. Talking to friends who learned to surf in locations outside of Baja has me excited enough to contemplate trying surfing again someplace else. After all, I was called a fish as a kid, learned to water ski when I was five, and love the water.

I hoped boogie boarding would become my water sport of choice for the Pacific side of Baja. Before moving to Todos Santos I had visited five months earlier, with boogie boarding at Cerritos Beach being one of the activities. At that time, it did not seem like the ocean was something to fear. With more time spent in the water after moving to the area, it was easy to see the waves at Cerritos are powerful on most days, which is why those who know how to surf love it. Waves and undertow were so intense I refused to boogie board or swim by myself. I understand and respect the power of Mother Nature too much to tempt fate. I can count on one hand how many times I bothered going to that beach by myself. Unfortunately, my time in the water was relegated to when someone was visiting. This was one of the drawbacks to Todos Santos, being in a beach community without the ability to be in the water whenever I wanted to. In fact, the beaches in Todos Santos proper had such a nasty rip current that seldom was anyone in the water along that massive stretch of sand. I certainly never was, and I am a fairly strong swimmer. What it meant, though, was fewer people in general were on the Todos Santos beach. This is a huge swath of warm, soft sand that goes on for miles. It was perfect for dog walking and contemplating one's future. I left the surfing to those who can read a wave and know how it is going to break.

The website Surf-Forecast.com says this about Cerritos Beach, "Playa Los Cerritos in Baja Sur is an exposed beach and point break that has pretty consistent surf. Winter is the best time of year for surfing here. The best wind direction is from the east. Tends to receive distant groundswells and the best swell direction is from the northwest. The beach break offers both left and right hand waves. Good surf at all stages of the tide. When the surf is up, it can get quite busy in the water. Watch out for rocks."

This spot is good for long boarders. The surfers who know what they are doing go farther out than rookies and are much closer to the rocks. Sitting on the beach watching them tame the waves can be mesmerizing. When the waves are taller than the surfers the athleticism is captivating even when the wave wins. La Pastora, north of downtown Todos Santos, is one of the spots where advanced riders go. The right-hand point break is known for having triple overheads or being about fifteen feet high. San Pedrito, a rockier location, is closer to Cerritos. These waves were popular with campers because it is possible to pitch a tent in the sand or be parked in a camper just feet from the water.

# Playing Concierge

Plenty of people arrived wanting suggestions for what to do, to know what I considered must-sees, where to dine, and any other information they could pull from me. The Tahoe room came with a three-inch thick binder full of more ideas than anyone could do in a month, let alone a long weekend. It started with the basic house rules so everyone staying could see them in case the person booking the room had not shared what was online. Unplugging was not what most people wanted to do based on the WiFi code being the first thing almost everyone asked for. This, too, was in the book. The book was predominately about where to play during their stay. A multitude of stories I had written for *Lake Tahoe News* about outdoor adventures filled the pages. This was better than a bunch of brochures that are only about selling people on some activity. That type of information is so impersonal and something they could pick up around town. Providing materials from random places would likely be an unintended endorsement, which I shied away from when it came to activities, restaurants, or rentals like boats or skis. I wanted to share my fun experiences in hopes it would give them ideas about where to hike, bike, snowshoe, cross country ski, paddle, as well as where to book helicopter and glider rides, along with what mansions to visit, other historical points of interest, and so much more. With each entry written in narrative form, this made the information more fun to peruse than a normal guidebook because these were stories instead of lists of facts. Color photographs added to the appeal and helped entice people to begin their own adventures. I included free postcards (an idea from a friend) so they could brag to others about where they had been. While it would have been exhausting to read the book cover-to-cover, many guests spent a good deal of time flipping through the pages.

Guests shared how enthralled they were with the binder of information, saying how they wanted to keep reading about the adventures when they knew they should be out exploring. In many ways this was like the bible to the great outdoors of Lake Tahoe and the surrounding area. When I was putting the book together, I did not anticipate it would be something that would set me apart from other hosts. Veteran Tahoe visitors as well as newbies to the area raved about it in person. It was also something many people mentioned in their reviews on the Airbnb site. Guests wrote: "We appreciated her suggestions for hiking, and the large binder of information she left in the room." "Kae was very helpful with giving us tips about our plans for our few days there and leading us to the best local restaurants for food. In addition, I so enjoyed thumbing through her notebook of her and AJ's hikes and adventures prior to going to sleep." "Kae was very accommodating and helpful, giving us tips on where to go and where to eat. She even provided a whole guide book on how to enjoy her house as well explore the sights in Tahoe, which we very much appreciated." "She patiently waited for us to arrive as we were driving through a snow storm. She knows all the trails and hot spots of the area, so if [you] ever need a suggestion, check out her handy guest binder."

People also had a chance to comment just to me in the guestbook that was in the room. "Thank you for all the information and articles to make sure we visited all the best spots around the lake." "Thank you so much for your hiking tips and all the information you left us in the binder—we are so lucky to have such a knowledgeable host!" "The book is a fabulous idea + chock full of ideas." "Thanks, too, for the detailed, first person narratives of all your travels that are found in the notebook." "Staying with Kae means staying with one of the most knowledgeable and articulate hosts in the area. Through her media business she has covered a lot of nature adventures and local businesses. She pointed us into right directions, and her binder provides more background information." "Kae was very flexible, relaxed, and fun to talk to. And, because Kae is so active, she had assembled a fantastic and detailed adventure library for her guests. We didn't take advantage of it this time, but it is a great resource for guests!"

A book like this is something every host should create, though copying what others have written without their permission could get them into trouble with copyright regulations. Once I put some of my hiking and snowshoe excursions into published books, my words could easily find their way to guest rooms throughout the Tahoe region. While plenty of travelers are content to do the most touristy things or follow a traditional guidebook, there are so many more who want to go off the beaten path. They want to know where locals go, what a local would recommend. This is certainly how I like to travel, by personal recommendation. When I gave up hosting in Tahoe my ex inherited the guidebook to regale her guests with. She added a few of her stories to the tome and put her personal touch on it.

Airbnb eventually created a space on rental listings where people could build an online guidebook. I never did. I did not want to share everything with the world or have other hosts poach what I had. Nor did I want people who were not staying with me to be able to cut and paste what I had written. This was long before I ever had the idea of turning many of those stories into hiking and snowshoe books. I am sure online guidebooks help the planners figure out what to do ahead of time. My guests had to wait for my ideas.

Another addition during my time as a host was Airbnb Experiences. One does not have to be a host or a guest to be part of the Experiences. Anyone could create an Experience, and someone not traveling could participate in one. The possibilities are as creative as the lodging guests provide. For a while, the best-selling Experiences, according to Airbnb, were Sangria and Secrets with Drag Queens, Cook Mexican Street Tacos with a Pro Chef, and Living Room Legends Scavenger Hunt Game. My plan for summer-fall 2020 was to create an Experience in the Tahoe area involving hikes that could be found in my books. The whole goal was to find another way to promote and sell my books. I had not figured out all the particulars before COVID-19 struck. While I continued to hike in Tahoe during the pandemic, doing so with strangers six feet apart did not seem like a fun idea nor did I want to be the mask police. If someone came down with the deadly virus, I did not want to be liable or have to go to court to defend myself. Plus, Tahoe was so busy that summer with people escaping the congestion of cities and suburbs, the last thing I wanted was to contribute to the chaos in the basin.

Having never lived in Todos Santos and having only visited once before moving there I did not have the same wealth of information to share with guests, at least not at the get-go. I took a binder with me in hopes of assembling useful reference material. It did not take long to gather brochures from outfitters with whom I had personal experiences. One was from my trip to Isla Espíritu Santo off the coast of La Paz on the Sea of Cortez side of Baja to swim with sea lions. This was an excursion that was at the top of my to-do list when guests wanted ideas. In addition to being a national park, in 1995 UNESCO declared it a world heritage site and biosphere reserve. Riding along in a *panga* with a handful of other passengers we saw a blue-footed booby on Seagull Island. So much for needing to go to the Galapagos Islands. There are more than one thousand islands in the Sea of Cortez, so exploring could go on for months. A free activity closer to the house that delighted everyone who experienced it was the baby turtle release, which happens from about October to May in Todos Santos. People at the releases become like a cheer squad, rooting for turtles to make it to the water with the hope they survive for years to come. Just to get to the ocean is hard work for these hatchlings that are only a few inches long. The initial wave tosses so many of them onto their backs, with them then squirming to get their footing. They must be dizzy and exhausted before the real journey begins. If it were not for the volunteers running the various turtle organizations, the future of these animals would be even more uncertain. Baja is home to five of the seven species of sea turtles in the world: leatherback, olive ridley, loggerhead, green, and hawksbill. Leatherback, olive ridley and green are found on the beaches of Todos Santos.

In-person discussions with guests in Mexico about what to do were the norm. Most had not been to Todos Santos, so any suggestion beyond what they found in their guidebook or on the internet was helpful. Once I started a blog in Mexico, I added my business card to the to-do book because the site featured many outings I thought guests would be interested in. Hiking adventures in the desert and the Sierra de la Laguna mountain range filled my website. Punto Lobos became my favorite hike near Todos Santos. At only about four miles round trip on an abandoned dirt road, anyone in decent shape could make the trek. The scenery on the route to this old fishermen's port is outstanding, with a three-hundred-and-sixty-degree view. Desert cacti dot the trail, with the blooms dependent on the season. The cove is rugged, making it obvious why it is no longer used. Sand stretches for miles up the coast. Turning around, the mountains loom in the distance. Picacho de la Laguna, the highest peak in the Sierra de la Laguna, is about seven thousand feet tall.

Mountain biking is huge in this area, with trails being created all the time. Cycling in the Punto Lobos area is also fun. While the water beckoned many to surf, fishing was a favorite pastime for some guests, whale watching was another, and swimming with the whale sharks is something everyone should do once. With Airbnb blocking all website exchanges between host and guest, it necessitated they go directly to my website for details instead of me providing them a link. No printer at the house also meant they had to put a little more effort into reading stories instead of merely opening a binder like the Tahoe guests could do.

Guests inevitably had questions, so expounding upon what was in either book was common. In Tahoe I shared my favorite hikes and snowshoes, where to grab a drink with a great sunset, which establishments had a good happy hour, and ones with a great fireplace. If someone was vegetarian or had some other food constraint, I could direct them accordingly. Some people needed specific details about where things were, though most relied on their phones or GPS in a vehicle to get around. Others came with no idea what to do so I became a personal concierge.

It was more than what to do that some people wanted assistance with. Big grocery stores did not exist in Todos Santos, so help with where to buy food was a common request. Names of stores were going to sound foreign, so even if they stopped in Cabo San Lucas before heading to my place, they would not intuitively know Chedraui was a grocery store and so much more. Plenty of people opted to eat in while at the Mexico house. After all, they had an entire kitchen without any rules as to what could be cooked. Within walking distance was a wonderful produce stand. I rarely bought veggies or fruit anyplace else. Along the same street was the best place for flour tortillas. If my sister had not told me about it, I am not sure how long it would have taken me to enter this tiny little market. It was half built, with re-bar sticking out from the concrete on what one day could be the second story. A dog often paced back and forth from that perch. No barrier prevented it from leaping to the pavement. In the back near the cash register is where the tortilla making took place. I am sure this operation would never pass any sanitary codes in the United States. It did not matter. I have never had a better tortilla than the ones that come from California Star. They are thin and light, without preservatives and whatever additive makes the ones in the U.S. so chewy. Eating them without any filling was a common snack, as was heating them up and adding a few drops of hot sauce. Up the street in the other direction from the house was a small market called El Sol Dos. This is where I sent people to get everything but produce. For its size it was amazing how much was packed into it. It helped that aisles are not as wide as what you find in the United States and some shelves are higher than I was accustomed to. It offers a mix of traditional ingredients Mexicans use and goods the gringos want. While I was there the store expanded, which allowed them to bring in even more ingredients to cater to the growing population of transplants and tourists. This included a lot of ethnic food that was not Mexican related, like Asian and Italian ingredients, along with a ton of junk food. I chuckled at seeing Costco's Kirkland brand ingredients on the shelves. This saved people from the hour trip to the big box store in Cabo San Lucas. People apparently were willing to pay for marked up Costco products if they did not have to make that trip.

While many ate meals at the Mexico house, eating out was a must for everyone. Actual Mexican food in Baja is not the heavy, over-cheesed plates of food found in the United States. It is lighter, fresher, and tastes healthier. Plenty of non-Mexican food is available too, from Italian to French to a micro-brewery to vegetarian. The options for great food really are endless in the greater Todos Santos area, especially for those who enjoy seafood. It is fresh from either the Pacific Ocean or Sea of Cortez. Fish tacos are everywhere. Most places let the customer decide what to add to the fish—with cabbage, avocado, onions, peppers, limes, and salsa the norm. The first time I was with friends from the U.S. who ordered fish tacos we were at a restaurant in La Paz. We looked at each other like this cannot possibly be all they were going to get. Grilled fish sat on a tortilla of about the same color, making dinner look so unappetizing. At that point they were jealous of my salad. The waiter could tell we were a bit perplexed. We probably confused him by staying seated. All the condiments were in a self-serve bar in the middle of the restaurant. Bland and boring became tasty and scrumptious. It was another learning experience, of which there were many in Mexico.

It was the rare visitor to Mexico who did not engage me about what brought me to the area and why the house was for sale. The latter was simple: my brother-in-law was done with Mexico, the family was not using it as a group, and it was time for him and my sister to have their money invested elsewhere or in cash so they could do other things. How did I get there? Pretty simple, too. I was tired of the cold and snow of Tahoe, had sold my house there in March 2018, and closed my business that summer. Initially, I was going to buy an RV, travel, write, and decompress after nine years of having a seven-day-a-week job. Then I visited Todos Santos in April 2018 for the first time to help my sister clean the house after full-time renters had vacated. We started talking about this empty house she was going to have—all 2,100 square feet. The following September we drove down together in a Jeep filled to the roof with my belongings and just enough space for AJ the dog. So began my adventure of being an expat. We struck a deal where I would live for free in the top part of the house while making money off Airbnb on the bottom part of the house. That money would be redirected to them to help defray their annual expenses of a second home or however they chose to spend it.

# Lights On

Dave and his bride, his description, were in Tahoe from the Philippines on their honeymoon. They had a penchant for turning on all the lights. One night I arrived home to find they were in bed, but every light except the ones in my bedroom and bathroom were on. (I kept my office door locked. This was where my computer, cash and other valuables like my tennis rackets were. Initially, I put what little jewelry I had behind those closed doors. I intentionally stopped that after I kept forgetting to.) The next night they added my bathroom to their list of lights that needed to be on. It was one thing to light up the house while they were in it, but the need to do so when they were not benefitting from it was unexplainable. At times like this I envisioned the dial on the electric meter spinning in circles so fast it was like watching money being siphoned from my bank account. I do not know if people were deliberately disrespectful, clueless or had some fear of the dark that necessitated needing the lights on. Multiple guests turned on more lights than the ones they were using. I am sure my quick finger on the off switch goes back to my childhood when my dad admonished me and my sisters when we left a room with the light on. It did not matter if we were returning there in a few minutes, he wanted the lights off if we were not using them. I am almost as obsessive as he was. I rationalized they would be less offended if I turned the lights off than if I asked them not to leave them on. I did not want to be confrontational with paying guests.

Sometimes I wondered if it were a cultural custom to have all the lights on. Another question I did not want to ask. All ages were electricity hogs. Luckily, it was not all guests. But my passive-aggressive way of handling the light situation usually did not get the message across. Even though I do not like lights on when they are not being used, I would leave a light on for guests arriving late or who were out longer than me or were arriving after I was in bed. I was surprised to have it still be on when I got up in the morning and the guest was home. Friends said I was expecting too much to assume they would turn it off. They were leaving things as they found it. I learned to message them that a light was on inside, please turn it off before going to bed. That was all it took—being direct.

While I normally stayed out of the downstairs quarters at Todos Santos when guests were out exploring, that protocol changed when lights were left on during the day. It was wasteful. Just in case someone had stayed behind I always knocked and shouted a warm "hello" as I opened the door. I did not want either of us to be surprised. No one was ever there. It was just a house all aglow. I do not know if they ever noticed the lights were off when they returned; no one ever said anything to me. I wish I could have gone around flipping light switches off at night in Mexico. I shook my head when I knew only one in the group of four was home, but lights in both bedrooms, the kitchen, living room and outside area were illuminated. On at least one occasion the lone person was on the couch as I walked by.

## Feeding the Ego

In the Tahoe room a guestbook was provided for people to make comments. These often went beyond what was written in a public review. No questions to prompt responses, which is how Airbnb would go about soliciting feedback for reviews. These were authentic thoughts written the old-fashioned way, with a pen on paper. They definitely stroked my ego. They made me realize how a guest be it friend or stranger likes to hear about your stay. Now I never pass on the opportunity to jot a note in a guestbook; at the very least to thank my hosts for sharing their home with me. Airbnb reviews as guest and host stick with a person's profile as long as they keep it active. My guestbook is something I will always have, whereas that is not necessarily true of any online review. Plus, the book is tangible. It is not something other than when writing this book that I read again, but knowing it exists brings back good memories of the whole hosting experience.

Some of the Tahoe guestbook comments went like this: "Thank you for always making sure we had what we needed and knew the best local places to go." "You were nothing but a wonderful host. We really enjoyed staying here and you made our first Airbnb stay perfect." "Also, we enjoyed the hot tub a ton, especially under the stars with a glass of wine." "From the moment that we booked our stay to the minute we left, you and AJ were very welcoming hosts." "Your house is absolutely adorable. Keep doing what you're doing." "We hope your work-life balance continues along the right path and that the Airbnb experience also continues to succeed." "We loved the coffee at your place and the comfortable bedding, it was much needed after a tiring day." "Quite honestly the best Airbnb we've been to yet." "You are such a beautiful person with an equally beautiful, accommodating home."

I left a similar guestbook on the coffee table in Mexico that was never used for its intended purpose. Instead, people literally treated it like scrap paper. The front page of each book said what it was to subtly nudge guests to leave a comment, so it is not like any guessing was needed to know what do with it. I envisioned the books to be a resource for future guests to learn about fellow travelers' favorite restaurants, where they went, suggestions for places to visit, even potentially ideas about things to avoid. All those things are what I find useful when reading guestbooks on my travels. I hoped people would offer ideas I had not suggested. Even contradicting my recommendations would have given people other opinions to consider. On my friend, Penny's, second trip to Todos Santos she got the comments started. It stopped with her. The next people used the book to keep score for games. This is what the book turned into until I gave up by removing it. I used it for other things not Airbnb oriented. I still wonder what the difference was; why in one location people wrote comments, and in another they chose not to. Perhaps the intimacy of staying in a room down the hall from me gave them more of a connection compared to the more remoteness in Mexico, even though I was just upstairs.

It was much like trying to figure out which guest was going to leave a review and scratching my head when someone stayed silent. With reviews being such a large component of the Airbnb world for guests and hosts, there were times when I was surprised by who did not leave one, and relieved when others skipped the process. I believe it is a host's obligation to be honest about her experiences with a guest so the next host will know what to expect. The best thing I could say is I would want the person back. A few times I left no review. This was the decision when I had been annoyed for the whole stay, rather than the guests doing anything egregious. My inability to handle their incessant talking or playing the same music repeatedly, or bristling because all the lights were left on when they were out might not register on the irritation scale with others. I did not want to give demerit points for things that some might see as an amusing quirk.

Admittedly, I was a bit obsessed with wanting good reviews. The website Review Trackers confirmed my need to pay attention to what others had to say. Their data says:

- Ninety-four percent of consumers say an online review has convinced them to avoid a business.
- People do not trust businesses with lower than 4-star ratings.
- Eighty percent of consumers say the star ratings they trust the most are 4.0, 4.5, and 5 stars.

Airbnb hosts could not remove a guest's review, which makes sense. However, there were channels to go through on the Airbnb website to dispute what someone said. While I did not always agree with what someone had to say, nothing was ever so out of line I felt the need to challenge their experience. My only interaction with Airbnb over a review was with Karen, the woman who did not stay, but whose family members did, and she still wanted to write something. Fortunately, I won that battle. One of my most favorite Mexico guests wrote what at the time I thought was such an ordinary review. "Beautiful home and perfect location. Kathryn was an excellent host!" Normally, I would have been thrilled and more than satisfied with those two sentences. Not that time. I was hurt and disappointed based on the connection I had with the wife and dad. My notes afterward said, "They were some of the best guests I had. I gave them a glowing review. What I got back was so damn ordinary. I guess I wasn't that special to them." In fact, this is the review I left: "Wow! These truly were the best guests I've had and not just because they shared their delicious food with me. No drama. Clean. Quiet. Fun to talk to. The eight days whizzed by. I would welcome them all back any time."

The wife and I had great conversations, mostly about food. It made me feel bad that the kitchen did not come equipped with much in terms of food staples or an array of pans. No complaints from her, though. Her dad said very little, even when he was on my massage table. As a certified massage therapist, in-room/in-house massage was a service I offered guests at both locations at my normal rates without the travel fee. In Tahoe that was $80 an hour, in Todos Santos it dropped to $50 an hour. Both were the going rates in their respective locations. Normally I only massage people in my home who I know, not strangers. It is ironic knowing I thought it was too risky to invite strangers to my Tahoe home for a massage, but I would let them pay me to sleep there. Airbnb guests as massage clients seemed like working on people a couple steps removed from being total strangers. They were already in the house, so there seemed to be little danger. Plus, I had all their contact information through Airbnb, so that gave me some sense of assurance I would have some recourse if things went sideways.

Massage school instructors trained us to flip a person off the table and run if we felt threatened. It was doubtful a naked client would chase after the therapist, but I have never needed to test this theory. Going to someone's house would normally be another $50 in Tahoe. Add snow or significant distance and the price went up even more to pay for my time and their convenience. In between my first and second seasons in Baja I took the table back to my storage facility in the United States. There was not enough business because I was not able to advertise or promote myself in any profitable manner since I was not legally supposed to work in Mexico. I did not have the proper paperwork. Much like non-citizens in the United States needing a green card or some other documentation to work, Mexico has similar requirements. With how difficult it was to fit the table into my Jeep Wrangler, I knew if I could take it back before my final trip, the easier it would be when that day came. Little did I anticipate I would spend another winter in Baja not at my sister's place—which eventually sold—and that I would take the table back down to use as payment to stay in my friends' casita.

The husband of this trio with the questionable review made the booking, so he was the one to write what they or at least he thought of me and the house. In retrospect, his review was much like his personality; quiet, to the point, not effusive. This dude was so quiet he initially came across as uninteresting, making me wonder how he and this dynamic woman were a couple. She sparkled. In hindsight I wondered if he might have seen her as overbearing and a handful. As a guest for a week, she was wonderful. I am guessing she liked having someone who allowed her all the attention without being jealous, someone who seemed accommodating to her. Maybe he was super interesting, but she was so domineering that in a short time span it was too hard for me to get to know him. I should not have been so quick to judge the review and them based on limited interactions. It is possible after a while she may have been too much for me to handle and he would have been perfect.

That is the thing about being a guest or host, you are part of people's lives for such a limited period of time. The interactions, though, can be powerful. I did not appreciate that as much as I should have. I probably had more power than I realized to make someone's vacation good or bad. If I were to be a host again, I would be a bit more altruistic in my approach to the business. It would be less about the money and reviews and more about trying to ensure people have the best experience possible. After all, I was living in two incredible places in the world that people clearly wanted to vacation in. It was just hard in the moment to always be magnanimous, especially toward the guests I did not want to see again.

This dynamic woman, though, would be welcome back as would her husband and dad. While people had left food behind before, she was the first to cook for me. They said they had plenty of food and wanted to share, and even delivered it upstairs where I lived. The melding of flavors was outrageously delicious. Sweet potato, black beans, cabbage, cilantro, avocado, olives—the mix of flavors was wonderful. It was a burrito bowl without a tortilla. While the dish sounds simple, it was the spices (I wish I had asked what she used) that brought it all together. What I learned in Mexico is how a squeeze of lime can do so much for many dishes. I used to be a lemon girl but switched to those tiny key limes that are about the size of a ping pong ball. They are the same ones that make for the best margaritas. This woman prided herself on being a bit of a foodie, asking me about places to eat and wondering why I had never been to Jazamango in Todos Santos. At first, I was not sure what or where it was. Then it hit me. That is the restaurant tied to the controversial Tres Santos development. I would never go.

Part of me wanted to inform her about the history of the restaurant, to tell her to watch "Patrimonio", the documentary about the destruction of the fishermen's lagoon, how big money tried to add five thousand homes to this town of six thousand people. Angst over broken promises lingers still in Todos Santos. Memories have not completely faded. Plenty of people remember what the greedy developers and their backers did and wanted to do. The controversy united gringos and locals, while it divided other families and friends. I did not want my political or social beliefs to influence or interfere with an Airbnb reservation or visit. I opted to stay silent about why I would never experience

70

Jazamango. I was not going to instigate a potentially controversial conversation. Even when guests would bring up politically sensitive topics, I was cautious about being too forthcoming with my opinions. Unless a town has a known controversial or historically significant claim to fame (something like a Civil War site in the United States), most tourists are oblivious. I do not believe it is a host's job to educate beyond the surface level unless asked. It was not like there was criminal activity going on there or that it was built with blood money. I also had to contend with the Mexico house not being mine and it was for sale. For my sister and brother-in-law's sake I could not get mouthy even if I had wanted to, even knowing at least my sister shared the same views about Tres Santos as I did.

While I did not get the stunning review from this trio that I had hoped for, plenty of other guests met or exceeded my expectations: "Kae was a great host! If we wanted to have a conversation she was a very willing listener and at the same time we hardly knew she was home. We felt a real sense of privacy." "Kathryn's house is beautiful. Nice big kitchen, big beds and amazing rooftop view of the sunset." "Nice touches with the beach chairs and umbrella. The outside eating area was really nice on those lovely evenings. Overall we were really happy staying here and the photos really depict what the place looks like except it is actually probably nicer." "A wonderful quiet oasis. Perfectly clean and a relaxing space. Good books and kitchen area." "And the shower was the best in all of Mexico - great water pressure and instantly hot."

By the end of my run as an Airbnb host, I had 117 guest reviews. Ninety-three of the 112 reservations in Lake Tahoe ended in a review, with twenty-four out of twenty-six Todos Santos bookings coming with a review.

71

# Arrivals and Departures

Early check-ins and late checkouts are common requests from people staying at a hotel. I have enjoyed both. Sometimes I arrive at my destination sooner than the scheduled time and have nowhere else I want to be. Other times I am done traveling and my room is where I want to land. In the morning I might not be in a rush to hit the road, and maybe want to spend a little extra time doing something fun in the town I was visiting so I asked for a late checkout. I should have anticipated Airbnb guests would want the same privileges. Now I understand how it can be such an inconvenience for the lodging establishment. It took being on the other side to finally respect the time it takes between guests for a place to be ready. Now I appreciate those establishments have employees who are on a schedule that I am asking to disrupt.

If no one was coming that same night and I was not planning to clean right when they left, another hour or two was not going to negatively impact my life. That is why it never hurts to ask for some leeway with the times. There were plenty of instances when it was no big deal. I did not hesitate to accommodate a late checkout/early check-in when guests were sufficiently spaced apart. A few times at both locations I let people keep their belongings at the house to retrieve after they checked out. It made sense they would want to milk as much time out of their vacation as possible—even on a short weekend getaway. The same was true on the other end with letting people drop off luggage before the check-in time. But if the host says there is no wriggle room with the departure or arrival time, honor it. Those back-to-back bookings at both of my rentals could be brutal. I had four hours to get the place ready if people left at the last minute and arrived right when they were allowed to.

Arriving early or leaving late without communicating ahead of time was always annoying. Check-in at both places started at 3 p.m. One time in Tahoe guys arrived before noon. The place was ready, but I was working and wanted some quiet time in the house. They were going to have to pay for another night if they wanted to come in. They chose to come back at the correct time. Had they asked ahead of time I probably would have said it was fine to arrive early. With advance notice, I would have at least let them drop off their stuff, then come back at the actual check in time. It is easy to work with people who respect you, your time, and your home. The others, well, it was just as easy to be obstinate. These two said they were unaware of the check-in time. This was just another example of how so many guests did not bother to read everything about the property. Check-in and checkout times are pretty basic, with all establishments having them. Red flags always went off when I knew they did not know the basic house rules. It inevitably ended up feeling like a long stay even when it was just a night.

I thought the checkout time of 11 a.m. on both listings was more than generous. Plenty of time to have breakfast at the house or go out, even time for a jog or to see something touristy close to the house. It was certainly enough time for a shower before hitting the road. Only a handful of people left after eleven o'clock. I learned after having a couple stay more than thirty minutes past checkout time to make my presence known to get them to pay attention to the clock. For stragglers in Tahoe who did not look like they were making any movement to leave, a half hour before their deadline to leave I would remind them about the checkout time. Some acted surprised (who knows if they were faking that reaction), others said no need to worry, they would be out. In Mexico I would knock on the outside door to share the departure rules if movement to pack up was not obvious. I was like the housekeeper at a hotel who knocks on the door while you are still in the room to give you a little nudge to move faster.

Airbnb allows hosts a tremendous amount of flexibility with being able to set the arrival and departure times. Most people offer a reasonable window for guests to come and go. Plenty do not want people coming at all hours of the day or night. That never bothered me. In Tahoe I did not care when people arrived. I learned that if they arrived after I was in bed, then that was one less night of having to interact with them. It felt like getting paid for nothing. If they ever added up the hours for that first night, they may have felt a bit fleeced. Essentially, they were paying only to sleep for that first night. I would like to think I would have heard the back door open or hot tub cover raised or shut if they ever used it on one of those late night/early morning arrivals. I never heard anything, which meant I kept sleeping but also that I had no idea what was going on at my own house. Nor did I always hear the front door. Arriving after midnight occurred more often than I anticipated but made so much sense with the bulk of the guests coming from the San Francisco area. They waited until they got off work to head for the mountains. On a Friday night what should normally be a four-hour drive could easily be doubled because of commuter traffic and Tahoe-bound travelers. Add in a holiday or a snowstorm and it would be an even longer drive. While I did not always like a ton of electronic conversation, I was grateful to the guests who kept me abreast of their estimated arrival time. Driving in the mountains can be treacherous. When more than an hour passed after they should have been in the driveway, I would send an email asking if they were OK. Most quickly responded to say there was traffic, they stopped for dinner, got a late start or whatever the reason was. Usually, they thanked me for checking in on them. It was a personal touch that I have never received from a hotel. I left a light on in the living room and one in their bedroom if they were arriving in the dark. It was amazing how quiet and considerate people were. Most people treated the sanctity of my home like they would want theirs to be treated—with respect. This meant being quiet when others are sleeping. Good communication and how loud or quiet people were ended up in reviews. Airbnb would also ask some specific questions in this regard as well, so being considerate mattered beyond being a decent human being.

In Mexico I asked people to arrive before 6 p.m. With two of the streets being dirt, signage not the best, and no street numbers in Todos Santos, the goal was to get people to the house before dark. (Most houses have names there, not numbers.) Plus, it is not safe to drive at night in Mexico, and not for the reasons one might think. It is not bad guys or even getting stuck in the middle of nowhere, though those can be real concerns just as they are anywhere. Cows. That is why you do not drive substantive distance at night anywhere in Baja. Horses and goats are other livestock to watch out for. Sure, there are deer and other wildlife on roadways in the United States and in other countries that can severely damage a vehicle or worse, but they seem to be in designated areas. The threat in the U.S. is often for short spans, not for a continuous one-thousand-mile stretch like it is in Baja. Driving to Cabo San Lucas from Todos Santos I had to abruptly go from sixty-five miles per hour to zero. A whole tribe of goats was crossing the road, stopping traffic in both directions in broad daylight. Had it been night, I would not have seen them in time to be able to stop without carnage littering the road.

The front door lock systems at both locations allowed people to come and go without me needing to be there or for us to ever interact. The lock box in Tahoe gave them an actual key to the house, while access in Baja was via a four-digit code on the front door. One time in Tahoe I forgot the code. I had been using four-digit numbers that meant something to me like my birth year, month and date of birth, my mom's birth year, an old address. I started by writing it on a piece of paper so I did not have to remember it. Then the paper disappeared, my memory failed, and none of the codes worked. In the process of a locksmith retrieving the key the device was rendered unusable. I installed another box, touched up the paint ruined by the dismemberment of the first one and then started typing in the person's code on my phone calendar with their listing. I kept that recording mechanism for Mexico, though, I could have always looked back at their profile to find their phone number. Why I did not look back at the string of emails for the Tahoe renters to have figured out the code that went missing from my memory is beyond me. The locksmith never needed to be summoned if I had been thinking more clearly. The Tahoe lock was not easy to change so I often kept the same code for months at a time. I trusted no one was going to come back to see if the key was there so they could burglarize the house. I also hoped no one was out duplicating the key to return for nefarious reasons.

## Therapy on the Couch

I never knew what to expect when single guests arrived, no matter their gender. It was a different dynamic in the house with a couple, whether they were romantically involved or friends. Duos had each other to chat with. I became the partner in conversation with singles. Though plenty of times solo travelers wanted space to be alone, which at times was the reason they were on their own. Stan was a different specimen all together. After he stayed, I should have added therapist to the list of amenities.

Being alone was the last thing Stan needed, at least on the first of his three nights. I did not think he would hurt himself, but I knew I could not turn my back on him and go about my night. His sadness was practically palpable. Sometimes it is easier to unload with a stranger than it is with friends or family. I was his safe stranger. It felt right to listen and to offer advice when he asked for it. It was obvious he needed someone in that moment. It did not take long before he completely opened up. He was having woman problems and life issues. We chatted for hours in the living room, each occupying a couch. The only things missing were me taking notes and sending him off with a bill at the end of the session. I have no idea how long we were there, but it was the better part of the evening. He had my undivided attention. I even put the phone down to avoid checking emails, which also meant disconnecting from my all-consuming job. This was not something I often did. I felt like we should have hugged goodnight as we went to bed. There was a bond, if only for that moment in time. It was like I was his big sister, or maybe he saw me as a mother figure—after all, I was probably twenty-five years older than him.

He was completely caught off guard when his girlfriend ended their relationship. He admitted there were issues, but he did not think they were worth breaking up over. He still wanted the relationship even though he knew they were not right for each other. He thought with some changes it could work. Having ended a long-term relationship more than a year earlier, I offered what I could from that experience and my other life choices. He could not change this woman he loved no matter what he said or did. He could only change himself and how he reacted to whatever situation he found himself in and to whatever words were hurled his way. I smiled at the thought of how my hours in couples' therapy were benefitting someone else and realized aspects of it still resonated with me. I tried to show him how if there were so many problems today, they were only likely to increase through the years. It is easy to play the "only if" game: only if she would do this, only if she would do that. Often it is the person in the mirror who needs to change, if only it is changing his or her expectations. I encouraged him to be as honest in any future relationship as he was with me. It might be too late to rekindle the spark with this last woman, but he owed it to the next one to be honest with his feelings, desires, needs, as well as insecurities. If only it were that easy for all of us.

After that first night Stan and I did not see much of each other the rest of his stay. I do not know where he went or what he did. He did not seem to be avoiding me. It was more like there was little left to be said between us. Asking him how he was doing would have seemed trivial. No one gets over a lost love in one night. I did not want to make him feel self-conscious around me either. Stan had a lot to think about beyond the woman giving him so much angst. I am sure with it being December and the holidays around the corner this just added to his sadness. That time of year always seems to provide enough stress without added negative emotion.

Stan left a nice, rather ordinary review on the Airbnb platform: "Stay was great. Would definitely recommend to anybody that wants a nice place to stay in Tahoe." I understood not wanting to share feelings that his ex-girlfriend might read or write anything that could be misconstrued. His ex may not have known or cared he left for a long weekend. I wondered if he deliberately stayed with me, a single woman, to get his ex's attention. How was she going to know we only talked? He may have started off as using me in some nefarious way to get back at his ex, but he did not seem like that type of guy. But I will never know why he chose me and my room. What I know is he was a super nice guy who was heartbroken. In the private guestbook in the room he wrote, "This has been a very peaceful weekend that allowed me a lot of time to think and find peace. And <u>TRULY,</u> thank you for being kind enough to take time away from your work to talk with me about my situation. I will never forget your kindness. I have always had trouble opening up to people, and your openness to talking with me made me very happy when I was feeling so much turmoil inside." My public review of him said, "Stan was a wonderful guest. If every ABB'er were like him, everyone would be a host."

## Malfunctioning Appliances

Cold showers are the norm in Todos Santos during the hot, humid summer months. By October the humidity is starting to break, and a little warm water while showering can be appreciated. I had been turning the hot water on ever so slightly to take the chill off. It was weeks before I realized I did not actually have propane warmed water; it was the natural temperature out of the faucet. Unbeknownst to me the pilot light was out on the hot water heater. This became a regular occurrence until the whole unit was replaced the second season I was in Baja. This meant a few guests were taking cold showers as well. No one complained. If they had, I probably would have figured out the problem sooner. The water temp was so different in Todos Santos compared to the icy cold tap water of Tahoe that it actually felt warm, well, at least tepid. Tahoe's water out of the faucet is so cold that when drinking it you do not need ice cubes. Ironically, soon guests were commenting on the hot water in Todos Santos: "The bathroom is big and airy with very hot water." It is definitely needed in winter, even in the tropics.

The water heater at my sister and brother-in-law's was so temperamental that the slightest wind could extinguish the pilot light. The unit was located outside on the bottom level. The little shed it was in was directly below a window in the upstairs bedroom where I spent the bulk of my time. It emitted a gurgling sound like it was boiling, maybe becoming overheated. Other times the whole unit creaked even when it was not windy. It was as if it were laughing at me in some sinister way. Not sure what I did to anger the hot water god, but she was not happy. It was daunting and unnerving to hear these sounds at night; and it was only at night that this contraption seemed to come alive. What was she saying? Who was she angry with? It was like she was an old person, cranky and creaky, on her last breath. Maybe the irony is that the hot water heater did not like to be cold. I spent plenty of time during the day in bed on the computer or reading a book. Only silence from that cylinder appliance when the sun was shining. If it were to blow up, it was going to take the second floor and me with it. These were the thoughts that ran through my head. I hoped I would be asleep when this eruption occurred, that it would be over fast and not be painful. I never shared my concerns with anyone. How does one rationally explain being scared of a hot water heater?

My sister had a neighbor getting paid to be the property manager. I took over some of the duties while I lived there. Asking for the pilot light to be ignited was getting to be such an annoyance that it was time to add this to my list of chores. Give me wood and fire any day; gas and fire I am not comfortable with. Success was achieved a few times, but it was getting old for everyone. Tim, the property manager, suggested a plumber look at the hot water heater. This dude cleaned the area around the pilot light and replaced something that was supposed to create a longer flame.

"Thank you for lighting the pilot. I actually had to light it on Saturday as well. It really is worse since the guy was out here. Whatever he did only exacerbated the problem," is the email I sent to Tim and copied my sister on in April 2019. Clearly, the hot water heater needed more than what this repairman came up with.

It got to the point that first thing in the morning I would test the hot water in the bathroom sink to know how my day was going to start: grab the lighter or do something fun. The day finally came when my scream was so loud the next-door neighbors came running. Flames shot out a couple feet, grazing my bare thighs. I have no idea if the blast blew me back or I jumped. My heart was racing. That would be the last time I attempted to light the heater. My neighbor, Andy, got it going that day as I was still trembling. Tim was summoned to resume the lighting duties until the heater was finally replaced.

The darn thing was probably the original heater when the house was built in 2006. Efficient it was not. When I left for four months the propane went from sixty-five percent full to fifty-five percent. Only the hot water heater was draining the gas during that time. It was dying a painful death. Finally, my sister made the decision to get a new hot water heater. When the guys came to replace it, they said they had never heard of the brand. That spoke volumes to me. Had the builder been trying to cut corners? While kitchen and laundry appliances are something I know a little about—at least with brands familiar in the United States—I am not well versed in hot water heater manufacturers. I could not tell you the name of the hot water heaters in the houses I have lived. I learned hot water heaters have a life expectancy of eight to twelve years. We were on year thirteen, so no wonder it was making noises. In November 2019 a forty-gallon Rheem was installed. A brand we had all heard of before. What a difference it

made. Hot showers even when it was hot out were a possibility. A pilot light that stayed on and a propane tank that did not
drain as quickly were welcome changes. It stayed lit even through
a tropical storm and other wind events. I do not know the price
tag for this apparatus or the installation expense, but my sister
and brother-in-law bought peace of mind for me, the neighbors,
guests and probably themselves.

Hot water in Tahoe was always necessary while showering
because what comes out of the tap is so frigid it would be like
taking a cold plunge. A furnace or some heating device was also
needed in the mountains, whereas heat in Todos Santos meant
adding a blanket to the bed or putting on a sweatshirt. A few
people had fireplaces in Mexico, but wood was so scarce it was
more of a decoration than anything useful. Modern air condition-
ing units in Mexico eventually came out with a heating element,
but these were things gringos opted for more than the locals and
were usually installed in new builds.

Overnight temperatures in the teens and twenties are common in the heart of winter in the Sierra Nevada mountains. To not
have a working heat source would be problematic. I learned the
hard way how people survived without central heat. It was New
Year's weekend, the Airbnb room was booked at a hefty price,
as was the norm during a holiday. Everything was ready for the
guests when the furnace started to sputter before going silent.
The fact that lighting a pilot light gives me trouble is a good indi-
cation that serious mechanical repairs are not part of my reper-
toire. This was going to be expensive, what with it being a weekend, a holiday, and snow was falling. If it were just me and the
dog, I would have opted for sleeping on the couch in front of the
wood stove. We might not have even noticed it was a cold house
since we liked it that way at night. Friends would certainly have

put us up, but could I bring the strangers with me? I could not even seriously fathom proposing that question to friends or suggesting the change in plans to guests. It is not like the guests on their own would be able to find some other place to stay in town. Christmas, New Year's, and Fourth of July are when all lodging in Lake Tahoe sells out.

I had to try to get the furnace repaired. Most calls went unanswered. Some shops could send a guy out after the holiday. Another would charge twice the normal fee for a visit, which was non-negotiable, and must be paid even if the problem was not fixed. I agreed to this extortion. I felt like I had no choice with paid guests in the house. A guy from one of the biggest heating companies in South Lake Tahoe diagnosed the problem, or thought he had, but said the shop did not have the part. How convenient for them because now they could charge me for another visit. In between calling repair people I secured a portable heater from my ex. This was the one person I knew who for certain had one. I fired it up and closed the bedroom door, knowing this would keep the guests more than comfortable. The wood stove was humming away, making most of the rest of the house cozy. Normally the wood was stacked neatly next to the stove, but knowing I would be going through more than usual, I set some on the carpet as neatly as possible. With the weather so crappy, I wanted to make sure the supply inside was dry so it could burn as hot as possible.

The guests were understanding of what was going on. They could tell I was working on the situation. It was an adventure to them, or so they said. Staying calm around them was my goal. Internally I was a basket case. I knew how cold the house could get at night. It was clear the odds of an immediate fix were diminishing. I was not sure how long they would see this as a fun, unique experience. An independent heating expert who was recommended from a friend who manages properties came out. He thought he could fix the heater, but also did not have the part. Parts were not available on a holiday weekend. They could not even be ordered. Brad did not want to be paid, saying he did not do anything that deserved payment. The other guy did not do anything either, but still took my credit card number. I remembered how Brad treated me when it came time to decide about the furnace.

2016 was starting off on a lousy note. That day and for the whole weekend the heater was not an option. It was not fixable. I willed myself to wake up every few hours to stoke the fire. Normally I would let it die out at night, then start the whole process over in the morning. Supplying fresh wood throughout the night kept the inside temperature tolerable. The guests never complained. They kept their room hot with the space heater.

In the coming days, with more eyes on the heater and explanations of what the replacement part might do, it was determined the life of this appliance was over. A new furnace was ordered, arriving long after those New Year's guests had checked out. Brad got the job, all because he did not gouge me on a holiday weekend. The other shop received a "professionally nasty" letter from me. I should have gone on Yelp. I never heard from them except to see the bill on my credit card. Like most repairs, there was more involved than taking out one unit and putting in the next. I trusted Brad to the point he was coming and going in the house to do duct work while I was in Utah on a working ski trip. That new furnace was ready for the next Airbnb'ers who arrived in mid-January. In addition to being warm with a flick of a switch, when the furnace came on it no longer sounded like a freight train was coming down the hall.

The guests did not even mention the furnace in their review or anything negative. I was so happy with their attitude during this whole experience that I made sure I called attention to their great attitudes. This is what I wrote about them, "Libby and Mike were wonderful guests. It was great to chat with them on the couch and as we roasted s'mores sitting in the snow around the fire pit. They were troopers with the furnace going out the day they arrived—New Year's Day. The wood stove, space heater and down comforter kept them comfortable! I look forward to their next visit."

Appliance malfunctions are stressful under the best of circumstances, but when paid guests are involved it goes way beyond the inconvenience factor and repair expense. People rightly expect certain basics when they travel like hot water, heat in the cold of a Tahoe winter, and refrigeration when a whole kitchen is provided. Add on that it is not your house so you cannot make the decisions, along with a language barrier, well, the stress meter accelerates upward rapidly with no kill switch. When the refrigerator went down, I had a six-hour window between when the repairman was to arrive and the guests could check in. What if he could not fix the refrigerator or it was not cold enough when the guests arrived? What if the repairman and I could not communicate since this was Mexico and my Spanish covered less than the basics? I would have to bring my mini fridge downstairs for the guests, then toss my Thanksgiving leftovers and other edibles into a compact cooler that was not going to be big enough for everything. Should I take a chance by putting the Bailey's on the counter at room temp? In that climate it seemed smarter to refrigerate it, but it was one of those Costco-size bottles I brought down as a treat. Such First World problems in a Third World country. Cold water was out of the question. Normally I kept a pitcher in the fridge because the potable water sat on the counter in a five-gallon jug. It was warm and not refreshing to drink at that temperature. I envisioned eating out for most of those five nights if I were going to have to live without real refrigeration. How people years ago functioned without this modern convenience is beyond me. I would not have made a good pioneer woman.

When I returned to Todos Santos in October 2019 after being in Tahoe for four months, the fridge was loud. I did not remember it sounding like that. At the same time, I was rarely downstairs, so maybe the motor had always made a bit of a ruckus. Maybe they make different noises south of the border. Maybe I should pay better attention. In November the motor no longer hummed. The fridge temperature hit fifty-something degrees Fahrenheit. The inside panel said the ideal temp was thirty-six degrees for the fridge, with the freezer at zero. I had not given up all hope because the freezer was keeping things frozen. Eventually the fridge hit seventy degrees. I moved what was perishable to the little refrigerator upstairs and hoped the rest survived.

This main refrigerator was less than eight months old. To sputter so soon was more than annoying. While it was under warranty, eventually I opted to have a local repairman look at it after dealing with Samsung for a week. Three service orders were placed with Samsung by phone and still no one had come to the house. One customer service person told me the repairman had been to the house. Not true, I told her. They had not even called to say they would not be coming. The last appointment was scheduled for the day after the guests' arrival. I did not want repair people in the house with guests for a non-emergency, though some would say not having a refrigerator was an emergency. I wrestled with whether I should let the guests know what was going on ahead of time. It would have been different if the appliance went out after their arrival. Having guests show up when I knew something was not working did not seem like a good business decision. That review would have been off the charts bad.

The decision to get a local guy out to the house also stemmed from the fact I did not trust the Samsung repair dudes to show up because they had already blown me off. I had spent two entire days at the house with the understanding they could arrive at any time. I did not want a third day tethered to the residence without results. *Mañana* was a common refrain in Baja. While the Mexican people are hardworking, industrious people, they do not like to say no, as in, "We will not be showing up today." It is always tomorrow, but you never know how many tomorrows you must go through before the actual one arrives.

Samsung was going to charge 700 pesos (about $35) just to drive to the house even if they did not fix the problem. I was told it was because of how far the house is from them—an hour or so whether they came from Los Cabos or La Paz. Bruno, the repair guy based in Todos Santos, charged 800 pesos (roughly $40) for his time and parts. He discovered water had frozen to the fan, causing it to shut down. He told me I had been keeping the refrigerator too cold. I had listened to what the Samsung people told me to set it at. Bruno informed me it cannot be that cold based on Todos Santos' climate. All the better he came out because the Samsung guys would inevitably set it at the colder temp, which might have entailed another merry-go-round with Samsung if the fan froze again. When Bruno left it was eighty-something degrees Fahrenheit in the fridge. Before the guests arrived, the fridge was at the desired coolness of forty-two degrees and the freezer at two degrees, and was keeping the ice as cubes and not water. The guests were none the wiser.

The only reason a new fridge was bought was to appease potential new owners. For those buying a house the appearance of appliances can matter. That is why during my first spring in the Todos Santos house a new refrigerator was ordered and delivered. My sister bought it the week she was in town that March.

It arrived on my watch. She and her husband had taken the advice of their new real estate agent to get rid of the old one. That one worked fine, but made the house look junky. It was a hideous white with scuff marks on the front that made you wonder how they got there. Making it stand out even more was that it was too small for the opening cut out in the countertops. The sleek stainless steel French door design of the new one fit perfectly and made the house be a true turnkey. The old one was something most buyers would probably have replaced immediately. This way they did not have that expense or trouble.

I would like to say that was the last of the refrigerator saga, but that was not the case. Somewhat fortunately for me it acted up again that December when my sister was back in town. She found out firsthand how difficult Samsung was to deal with. The hours she and I spent on the phone with a company representative was absurd. Eventually, though, the repairmen came out. No fee to drive to Todos Santos was mentioned. The part was replaced. Again, it was on a day Airbnb guests were arriving, just to add stress to my life. No problems after that visit. We went with their recommendation of temperature with the thinking it was still under warranty and better to do what the Samsung people said. Even so, I kept Bruno's number. At least he was respectful of my time, even if his initial repair was not enough to keep the refrigerator going.

## Absentee Host

Sandy contacted me wanting to stay that night with her boyfriend. Good thing the room was ready for others later in the week because normally I was not set up for spur-of-the-moment requests because their room was my room when it was just me. Based on my workweek and the distance between bookings it was sometimes easier and more convenient to stay in the little room so I knew the room would be ready for paid guests. While the last-minute booking seemed a little odd, Sandy had good reviews. They were traveling nurses headed to the San Francisco area.

AJ, who had let them in while I was out, was silent about what she thought about them, which was a good thing. I would have been worried if she had been acting weird. The next morning while they were having breakfast on the deck I popped my head outside to introduce myself since they were behind closed doors when I got in the previous evening. They wanted to stay another night, but it was blocked off on the online Airbnb calendar because I was supposed to be on a one-night get away with the dog to a resort less than an hour away. I won the stay in a raffle and the expiration date was nearing. I did not want to lose out on this rare opportunity to escape for a night. I trusted my gut and let them stay without me. I joked—sort of—to not burn down the house. They were probably as excited to have a house to themselves as I was to make money without being there. My only apprehension was knowing the internet and cell service were spotty at best where I was going. What if they needed to reach me? Oh, well. Time to put myself first. Usually, my business was the number one priority. I could already taste the blackberry cobbler and an adult beverage at the resort. This is not to say it was not weird to have strangers in my house without me. It was. But it was my choice, and usually my instincts are good. For the most part I successfully convinced myself to stop caring. I needed to unplug. Surprisingly, I was able to relax. Time in the hammock with a glass of wine after hiking new terrain was the recharge I needed. Even more shocking was not caring if news happened and some other media outlet got it first. I was that exhausted and burned out from being the sole proprietor of a 24/7 news site.

I was always curious about what went on in the house when I was gone, and not just this particular night. I never wanted to know what was happening in the bedroom. Noises were more than enough information. I wondered about more mundane matters like did they use the kitchen when they were not supposed to? Were their shoes on the couch? Mostly, it would have been interesting to know if the dog was behaving and were they treating her well. I never contemplated putting cameras in the house to keep an eye on the dog or the guests, or to see how they interacted together. I was not that curious. I would have used any incriminating photos if I had a camera or two or three, as documentation to prove they broke something or hurt AJ or whatever the infraction was. My biggest concern was the dog. I am glad I never felt the need to install cameras.

Airbnb has caught some flack at different times about hosts who have cameras. Eventually, they created a camera policy that said, "If you're a host and you have any type of security camera or other recording device in or around a listing, even if it's not turned on or hooked up, we require that you indicate its presence in your House Rules. We also require you to disclose if an active recording is taking place. If a host discloses the device after booking, Airbnb will allow the guest to cancel the reservation and receive a refund. Host cancellation penalties may apply." Rules do not stop people from misbehaving, it just means there can be consequences. Some hosts formed a Facebook group called Airbnb Guest Blacklist. It was full of pictures of guests, some comments including names, and some descriptions of why those guests should be banned. Even though this particular group was taken down, it was resurrected for a time and open to anyone. Now it is a private group with six thousand members. On the flip side, there is a private Facebook group called Airbnb Hosts Blacklist with forty-seven-hundred members. Several social media groups are designated solely for vacation home rental hosts. I could not imagine wanting to belong to a forum like this. Even misbehaving guests have a right to privacy.

Apparently, a night without me was to the nurses liking because they wanted to book another night even knowing I would be returning. I barely hit the approve button in time. Airbnb gives hosts twenty-four hours to respond before the request is denied for lack of response. Had this happened, it would have meant less money in the bank and being dinged by Airbnb. They pay attention to response times and include it in superhost criteria. This hosting thing really was a business and needed to be treated as such. Not having cell service could potentially be a problem going forward. Airbnb allows cohosts for situations like this. I was only in my second month being a host and was not ready to relinquish control or go with the instant booking option that Airbnb provided. Being a bit controlling meant never wanting a friend to decide who I would be sharing my home with.

Beyond being a delightful couple, they erased the bad mojo of Karen, the third-party booker and her dreadful relatives who never stayed. It was good to know my instincts were intact when it came to trusting people. Still, not being home when people were in my house was not something that happened on a regular basis. I really was not comfortable with people being in the house without me popping in now and then. A few times I never saw the guests because our schedules were such that we were only in the house at the same time to sleep. But at least they knew I was there or there were signs I had been there, like a fire was going or dishes were drying, or AJ was outside when she had been inside.

A few months after my one night of being gone with guests in the Tahoe house I created an Airbnb listing for the whole house. I planned to rent it when I left town. Maybe it would pay for my vacations. The first opportunity was over Thanksgiving. While this is a normal time to inflate the nightly price, the amount I came up with for the whole house was astronomical. I planned to use the office as the owner's space by locking it off. This would leave two bedrooms, with the possibility of two people in each room. I was sure others could fit in the living room if people wanted to. I wondered if I should take everything that meant something to me and put it in the office or garage. Suddenly, so much meant everything to me. Those cookbooks mom gave me that had been a wedding gift to her. The afghan my grandmother had made me. Gifts from friends. Do I move all my clothes? Do I trust books would not be permanently borrowed? Do I put a chain around the wood stove so it could not be used? While that was one of my favorite investments, it could become a tremendous liability.

I was such a nervous wreck with the thought of people renting my home I took the listing down before anyone even inquired about it. A second home or a house whose main purpose is to be a rental is one thing, but to rent out my primary home was too much for me. Beyond the cash, my imagination only went to negative possibilities. Plus, to be responsible, I really should have had a local property manager if I were going to be out of town. Eventually, South Lake Tahoe made that stipulation part of its vacation home rental ordinance.

# Limited Privacy

Pictures on the Todos Santos Airbnb listing showed the up-stairs deck area and one of the many gorgeous sunsets from that perch. Those who took me up on the suggestion of watching the sunset from there were never disappointed. Stunning hardly begins to describe the sunrises and sunsets in this part of the world. No one, at least while I was home, used the lounge chair. Plenty of people sat in the chairs looking out to the Pacific Ocean, which was a mile away. It was an ideal way to start the day with coffee or end the day with an adult beverage. Starting in October it is possible to see whales from this vantage point. The air they release looks like a spout of water spraying skyward. A whale's blowhole is the equivalent to a human's nostrils. With it on top of their head, there is no reason to lift their whole body out of the water. These mammals migrate from the frigid waters of Alaska to the warm waters of Baja to give birth. Some swim as far south as Colombia. In spring they make the return trip. Mostly it is humpback whales plying the waters of the Pacific Ocean. Some reports say ten thousand humpbacks migrate a year. Gray whales are the other most common visitors to the tip of Baja.

A more expansive viewing area was achieved by climbing the nearby spiral staircase. I tried to catch everyone before they went up or told them upon our initial meeting that only one person at a time could be on that wrought iron staircase. It was such a Mexico thing with the top not being fastened to the house. It fit into a groove cut into the brick. Had two people been on the stairs at the same time, it would be possible one could be bounced off to a painful or fatal landing. Once on top it was a three-hundred-and-sixty-degree view of the greater Todos Santos area. This was the best spot to be at sunset. The house was in a neighborhood slightly above sea level, which is why the views were so incredible with or without a sunset. Sunrises were awesome as well, but I stayed in bed to witness those or walked just outside my door if it were photo worthy. The light at dusk in this coastal-desert enclave could be extraordinary, casting colors often only found on a painter's palette. The pinks and purples spilling forth onto the surrounding mountains were mesmerizing. If clouds were near the horizon, the colors were even more magnificent. This view alone would have sold me on the house if I were in the market for a home in Todos Santos. It is where my sister and her family would always spend their first night. On that ledge atop the spiral staircase is where I spent my last night at the house soaking in memories and contemplating the future.

The first upstairs level was the entrance to my living quarters. No window in the entire house had coverings of any sort. In other words, I had little to no privacy when people would come to the upper deck. A few guests knocked on my door, wanting to talk to me. This always startled me because even with guests below me I expected them to communicate via the Airbnb app, or texting, or to flag me down as I wandered through their outside area as I was coming or going. With everything being concrete, I could not hear the rubber soles of shoes approaching. AJ was going deaf, so she never alerted me that someone was coming. I never shared that piece of information with guests, though I am sure they figured it out. No one ever knocked at an inappropriate hour, it was just that I stayed in bed long after most people were decently dressed and had started their day. When I became self-employed years ago, I learned I could begin my day in bed with the laptop. No reason to change this routine. Even without work, the computer was on my lap in bed to read the news, catch up on emails, and dabble on social media. Tennis was about the only thing that got me out of bed at what most people would call a reasonable hour. While I was never wearing skimpy pajamas in Baja, it was still nightwear. I did not have a robe to throw on. I could not dash into the walk-in closet to put on more appropriate clothes because they would see me through the window or door. At least what I had on covered everything. No one seemed too alarmed about my lack of appropriate attire, but no one lingered long either.

One knock came when I was on the toilet. My living area was an oversized bedroom, walk-in closet that doubled as my kitchen, and a bathroom that was open and did not have a door to it. The bathroom had a great layout where you walked around a barrier that was more than waist high. The toilet was next to this wall on the left. Then an expansive counter with a sink filled the rest of that wall. The walk-in shower was at the far end. It had concrete with decorative tiles in a tiered format as a wall to allow privacy while lathering up, but no door and no threshold to step over. It was one of the best designed bathrooms I have seen. That is until a stranger knocks on the door. I could not ignore the knock because the front doors were open, with the screen doors easy for them to talk through had they been so inclined. I said I would be right there. At least I had appropriate clothing on once I pulled up my shorts. I chose not to flush the toilet so they would not know what I had been doing, but I did wash my hands.

The most embarrassing guest encounter occurred early on when I walked from the shower to the bedroom without a towel around me just like I had done so many other times. My exhibitionist ways clearly followed me south of the border. I was oblivious to the fact that guests were outside on the upstairs deck until I saw them. I froze for what felt like minutes before instinctively dropping behind the side of the bed to hide. I would put money on it that two of them saw me, all of me. In what was probably a split second they turned around as quickly as I fell to the floor. Fortunately, I could pull all the clothing I needed from the dresser. Most of the time in Baja I was in shorts and a T-shirt. That day was no different. Getting dressed laying down and sitting so my head was not above the bed was a slight struggle but doable. The guests were gone when I ventured outside. Had they really seen me? Did I scare them away? Were they too embarrassed to talk to me now that they had seen more of me than they wanted? We never talked about it. Good thing. What would we have said? Maybe it made for an interesting story for them when they shared their Baja experience with friends. Luckily, the encounter did not end up in their review.

## Outdoor Meccas

South Lake Tahoe and Todos Santos are outdoor playgrounds, which means people bring gear with them or rent it while they are in the respective towns. Knowing this about Tahoe from the get-go made me think about what to do with all those toys people would be bringing with them. I did not want guests to have access to the garage because that is where all my sports equipment (except my tennis rackets) were stored. I am not sure if I was more worried about them taking something or leaving the door to the garage unlocked. When I rekeyed the house, I purposefully had the garage have a different key so guests would not have automatic access. In Baja, there was no garage. Tennis rackets were my only toys in Mexico and those easily fit in my closet.

House rules for Tahoe said all their gear had to stay outside. This meant no skis, snowboards, or bikes in the house. Because the house was mostly carpeted, I did not want water from winter toys or grease from summer ones damaging it. The few who asked to bring their boots inside I said yes to without hesitation. I understood how miserable it is to put on ice-cold ski boots. I had a hard enough time getting into mine when they were kept at room temperature overnight and then on the floorboard of the vehicle to warm up. The foyer was plenty long and wide enough to not trip over multiple pairs of boots. With the entry being tile, any water that dripped off them was not going to do any damage.

Unless someone snuck in ski gear that I never saw, everyone adhered to keeping it in or on their vehicle. I rationalized if they could get the equipment to Tahoe, there was no reason it could not stay where it was. While people still transported skis on exposed roof racks, so many more put them inside their vehicle or in an enclosed rooftop carrier. With skis and boards being locked out of sight, the odds of anything being stolen were slim. I did not want skis against a wall in the house where they could easily slide down, taking the paint with it, and damaging whatever they would land on. The bedroom wall was already getting dinged up from what I presumed were suitcases rubbing against it. I wish I had thought of putting luggage racks in the room. It was not a guarantee that luggage would not still hit the wall, but it might have lessened that likelihood. It also would have been a nice gesture. I knew the wicker trunk at the base of the bed was good for one suitcase, but I should have provided two places. My sister had those in place for both downstairs rooms in Todos Santos long before the house became an Airbnb rental.

Two-wheeled toys were something I had not given much thought to when I was making my Tahoe rules. Then I found a pair of high-end bikes locked to each other in my side yard. With nothing there to lock them to, it would be possible for a thief to carry them out even with a lock around them. Despite living in a safe neighborhood, I knew these needed to be more secure even though behind the fence they were not viewable from the street. The couple was visibly grateful to be able to store them in the garage. Who knows what I would have done if I did not like these two so much. I would like to think I would have made that same offer to anyone because it was the responsible thing to do. Right or wrong, I treated the people I liked better than the guests who irritated me. OK, so that is wrong in the service industry, but this was my home and my business. How was anyone going to know? Based on reviews I was a good actress when people bothered me because what they wrote made it sound like they were none the wiser.

Tahoe was making a name for herself as a mountain biking destination while I lived there. With the U.S. Forest Service owning about eighty percent of the land in the Lake Tahoe Basin, cyclists are usually on federal property. Plenty of forest to pedal through. Some is easy to moderate single track; even more of it is technical. Rocks and logs provide natural obstacles, while some were strategically placed during the trail building process. For those wanting to perfect their skills and work on jumps, South Lake Tahoe built a bike park that included a pump track. It has been a collaborative approach to improve the infrastructure for cyclists. Tahoe Area Mountain Biking Association (TAMBA) was formed in 1988 by Kathlee Martin and Jesse Desens in North Lake Tahoe and Gary Bell in South Lake Tahoe. It was resurrected by a group of mountain biking advocates in 2011 after going dormant in 2003. This was after the Forest Service and IMBA (International Mountain Biking Association) hosted the Tahoe Trails Conference in October 2010. Thus began a strong public-private partnership to maintain current trails, decommission some, and build miles of new ones. TAMBA has been so successful in its reincarnation that it has paid staff. Other organizations in the Tahoe-Truckee area are instrumental in trail building and maintenance as well. Max Jones, who is in the Mountain Bike Hall of Fame, is best known in the Tahoe basin for what he has done to promote the Flume Trail on the Nevada side. It is one of those rides where those with a fear of heights will not want to look down when the most scenic stretch unfolds along this fourteen-mile one-way ride that climbs to eight thousand feet.

These cycling guests were two twenty-something-year-olds from Davis, a college town near Sacramento that has a huge biking community, so it was not surprising they would have nice wheels. I explained the hole in the bedroom door, and they got it without any attitude whatsoever. They did not spend much time at the house. Instead, they were out helping the local economy and enjoying Tahoe by riding Heavenly Mountain Resort's gondola, spending time in Nevada at a popular beach, and dining at Blue Angel Café. The latter was my favorite restaurant on the South Shore of Tahoe, and where I always sent people. It was heartbreaking when it closed in summer 2019. This active couple mentioned how at Zephyr Cove Beach they steered clear of the area with all the young people. I smiled. I thought they were the young people. They biked to Cove East near my house and walked to dinner, then recovered by soaking in the hot tub. They made the most of their short time in Tahoe. If only all guests could have been like them. They were so easy to get along with, self-sufficient, considerate of my space by being clean and quiet, and totally embraced what Tahoe had to offer.

In Todos Santos it was mostly surfboards that people brought as their outdoor toys. Some flew with their boards; others rented them for multiple days once they got to Baja. Thefts in the area were often a crime of convenience. Even though the house had a gate, it did not have a lock. I never saw surfboards locked to a vehicle like you do with skis and bikes. I told people not to leave boards on their car roofs, and instead suggested a less obvious location on the property. Nothing was stolen on my watch. Some people kept their boards inside downstairs, which did not bother me. With the floors and walls concrete, the threat of damage was not the same as it was in Tahoe. The one couple who had bikes with them stored them inside at my urging. I did not want to dangle that valuable carrot to the crooks in town by leaving them outside or even on their truck.

With the surfboards came the wetsuits. At times the downstairs patio area looked like a yard sale with all the neoprene strewn about, along with towels and swimming suits. Other times wetsuits were hung on vehicles to dry. Sand was a constant—inside and outside the house, and definitely on the patio and front step. That is why a broom was left inside in a highly visible location. A hose on the side of the house could be used by these guests. The downstairs bathroom came with a spigot that was ideal for washing off feet as well. (It was also the perfect height to wash AJ.)

Beach chairs, boogie boards, beach towels, and a tiny cooler were in the downstairs large bedroom closet. They had been bought by my sister and brother-in-law for their family. I kept some of the toys in the private bodega for when friends came to visit. I had a lounge chair and a hammock at the house I could use if sunning was really of any interest. It never was. I got my tan by playing tennis and hiking. Beach time was really about dog walking. One group left a towel at a beach in La Paz, about an hour away. It would have cost more money in gas to retrieve it than it was worth. I was appreciative of their honesty, though I would have quickly discovered it was missing when I did laundry. While they were still there, I looked around Todos Santos for a beach towel, with the only place selling one for $40. It was not going to matter how plush of a towel it was, that was outrageous. I knew I could get one at Costco or Walmart in Cabo San Lucas for a reasonable price. The woman left a few pesos for a replacement. With the house for sale and other beach towels in the house, my sister said to not worry about replacing it. The important thing was I still had four available for the guests.

## Kitchen Escapades

People who expect a rental kitchen to be fully stocked like the one they have at home or for it to be even better can be disappointed. I am sure that was the case with the Mexico Airbnb listing. Because my sister does not drink coffee, she did not believe providing a coffeemaker was necessary. Even though I no longer drink coffee, making me a minority among my friends and probably much of the world, I disagreed with her decision. When friends visit me, my coffeemaker gets plugged in. Based on how much my Airbnb coffeemaker got used in Tahoe I knew it was a standard apparatus for most people. People even mentioned the in-room coffee pot in their reviews. Had the Mexico house not been for sale, and we thought this might be a multi-year gig, it would have been more logical to put a few if not several dollars into more kitchen basics. I could have overruled my sister by purchasing a coffeemaker, but I did not want to invest in the Mexico Airbnb because it was not completely mine.

Still, the listing was under my name, which meant all reviews were attached to my Airbnb profile, not my sister's. Reviews as a host and guest are available for anyone to see so it was in my best interest to get good reviews even if I never planned to host again. I do not know if my hosting reviews mattered to potential hosts, but they were there for the reading when I booked a place as a guest. I always found it interesting to read reviews of potential guests who were also hosts. It gave me insight into how they might treat my rentals as well as what they might expect. If someone kept being complimented on his rapid response time, I knew he would be a good communicator; while if the host was dinged for her lack of cleanliness, I knew it would take me longer than usual to clean when she was gone.

Besides reviews being a reason to want guests to have the amenities they deemed basic, I wanted them to be happy and have a great visit. Even so, putting cash into something that was always going to be temporary seemed like a poor investment. Starting out I had no idea how long I would be in Todos Santos considering the house was for sale. Nor did I know if this venture would be successful in terms of bookings and dollars. I naively thought the house would sell in a matter of months, even though it had been on the market for a while. The first season I was in Todos Santos ten months, returning the next fall for six more months. The house was not available on Airbnb when my sister or other family members were in town.

Naturally, the first guest inquired about a coffeemaker as soon as she got there. Even though the listing indicated there was no coffeemaker, I knew I had to remedy the situation. For those who need their caffeine fix, it would never cross their mind a house would not have a coffeemaker. Friends in Cabo San Lucas, which is about an hour south of Todos Santos, came to the rescue with an old one that was sitting in their garage. They even had a supply of filters. I bought coffee on my way back as a way of saying sorry all of this was not taken care of before they arrived. The guests were appreciative and said so in their review: "Kathryn was an amazing host. We had noticed there wasn't a coffeemaker and within the next few hours, she went out to get one, along with a bag of coffee & filters." Months later my friends needed their coffeemaker back. That is when my sister sprung for one, realizing even if we were never going to use it, it would be well used. I always made sure filters were on hand, with coffee being in the freezer most of the time. Decent coffee costs much less in Mexico than the United States. Sugar was in the fridge. They were on their own for cream, at least in Baja.

In Tahoe it was easy to keep the individual creamers stocked because I could buy them in bulk at Costco. I am not sure I would do that again because it creates so much unrecyclable waste. If I had a similar setup, I would probably provide the powder cream, knowing if they wanted something else they could stock it in the refrigerator. Those tiny creamers would not have lasted in the humid climate of Baja.

In Mexico the pans were a mishmash but were serviceable. At the start of the second season, I brought down a large stockpot my sister was not using at her main home. It was good for soups and cooking pasta. This was after a woman left a private comment for me saying the pans were lacking. "Kitchen needs bigger pots and pans, at least a couple," she wrote. She was cooking for four, so her needs were much greater than mine. I rarely cooked for anyone besides myself because it was hard to invite people over when I did not know if I would have access to the kitchen because of Airbnb'ers being on the premises. I had no problem breaking spaghetti in half to cook it in the smaller pot and never needed that much soup, so not having that larger pot the first winter was not an inconvenience for me. Even after that addition another woman said the kitchen was missing some basics but did not say what.

I was angry to discover one of the small pans had been scorched. After guests checked out, I never scrutinized the wear and tear on pans or other kitchen gadgets. Nor did I survey the inventory to see if something was missing or ruined. I should have. I scrubbed the best I could, but to no avail. It was disappointing the culprits did not own up to this damage. It would not have cost much to replace. By the time I wanted to use the pan a few people had been in and out of the house so I could not pinpoint who was responsible. This left me with zero recourse with Airbnb to file a claim or even question the culprits. The pan was still usable even though it did not look great. If it had been a pan in my kitchen, I would have replaced it. It was that bad. For a rental house that was for sale, the pan was going to have to suffice. One of the last comments was: "The price for the value was super over all, the only thing I would suggest—as others have—is that the kitchen really needs a decent set of pans as what was available was very limited and well used and only small pans." The pans were never upgraded. Little did I know after that comment there would be no more Airbnb renters. I headed back to the United States when COVID-19 hit in March 2020 and was never an Airbnb host there again.

The glasses in Mexico were an ensemble that did not match, which can almost seem trendy. I did not have a problem setting a table for eight the one time I had that many people for dinner. Silverware, plates, bowls—all plentiful. Basics like a colander, grater, measuring cups, knives, utensils, and serving dishes were all in the cupboards or on the counter. Silverware was more than sufficient. One of the problems with what was available is full-time renters had been at the house at varying times through the years. Even though my sister kept an inventory of what was in the house, things went missing, were broken, or not replaced. By the time I showed up it was not set up to be the perfect second home or rental. Considering the Airbnb price during non-holiday periods was $100 per night for four people, what the house came with was more than adequate.

The only thing I had upstairs in Baja they may have wanted was a microwave. I brought it from the United States knowing I would be reheating food while Airbnb'ers were in the house. I would like to think I would have felt a tad guilty had I pirated it from downstairs. But that would not have happened without my sister giving me the green light to do so. Eventually, it became a permanent Mexico appliance. I left it at my friends' casita for their guests to use after I called their place home one winter. They then gave it to their housekeeper. The blender in my pseudo-kitchen at my sister's came from a store in Mexico. I used it more than I expected. Smoothies, pesto, and soups were the main reasons it got fired up, and for the occasional blended margarita. That was usually when I added fresh mango to the tequila concoction. I took the blender back to the States for my mom who was replenishing kitchen items after being burned out of her home in the Camp Fire in Paradise, California, in 2018. I could see why a microwave and blender were not things my sister or brother-in-law cared about providing for people, as they could be deemed extras and not essentials. Based on how much I used both, especially the microwave, they are important in my culinary world. This must be the case for a lot of people considering it is usual for a built-in microwave to be part of home construction today. I also brought down an Instant Pot and later bought a hot air popcorn popper. I left the popper in the downstairs kitchen upon my departure.

Drinking water was something my sister and I did not know what to do about at first. What came out of the faucet was likely to make a person sick, even though I brushed my teeth with it and showered in it. While most full-time residents in Todos Santos pay for a water filtration system so they can consume the water out of the tap, my family was not going to pay for that feature on a house they did not intend to own much longer. I bought a package of one and one-half liter bottles of water with the intention this would be for the guests to start out with and then they would supply their own as needed. This was going to add up pricewise for whomever was paying the bill and certainly was not the eco-friendly solution. Before people arrived, I realized potable water is a basic necessity that needed to be supplied their entire visit. I certainly expect water at any rental I stayed at, be it Airbnb, hotel or someplace else. The house had a five-gallon refillable jug that was in a custom-made iron holder. The contraption allowed the bottle to tip easily, thus eliminating the need to lift it to pour. These bottles were heavy, weighing almost forty-two pounds when full. My sister asked the people she knew in town where to find a similar container. No ideas, as they had filtration systems. Between the time my sister went back to the United States and the first guests arrived, I found a pump that screwed onto the top of the water bottle. I used this in my living quarters upstairs, while the guests had the original water dispenser. This eliminated the need for constantly buying individual plastic bottles.

The first case of water did not go to waste, as I took most of them on the road when I traveled. I learned the hard way while traveling in Baja that not everyone thought potable water should be included in the nightly price. I bought an obscene number of small water bottles on excursions because the locals did not provide an alternative. In the U.S. I am used to refilling my water bottle. This was seldom an option in Mexico when I traveled.

106

I made it a point to refill that five-gallon bottle for my Airbnb guests as many times as they wanted. The more active people were, the more *agua* they consumed. Like me, they used it for all their cooking needs—pasta, rice, quinoa, coffee and who knows what else. I am guessing they used this "good" water to clean produce, too. I relied on Microdyn for washing my vegetables. I did not want to take the time to explain to people what that was for, instead deciding it was easier to keep refilling the big jug. A private message from a guest via Airbnb said, "Thank you for lifting all those bottles of water!" (Airbnb allows guests and hosts to write comments to each other that are not public.) The water facility was a storefront in downtown Todos Santos a little more than a mile from the house. This purification plant used a reverse osmosis water treatment system. Even in months where the house was full of guests more than it was empty, I never spent more than $4 on drinking water. AJ was drinking this "good" water, too, because she had a kidney disease, and I was afraid what came out of the faucet might make her sick. The people working at the water shop knew me as a regular, as I was there about every third day when guests were in the house. The bottles were rinsed out, then filled with fresh water, wiped off and carried to the Jeep.

When appropriate I was emphatic guests know the water shop closed on Sundays, so they needed to plan accordingly. That did not stop people from telling me late on Saturday they needed water. "We're big water drinkers," one woman said. I gave them a couple liters of that bottled water I had upstairs. They were going to have to fend for themselves until I could get the big one filled. More conscientious people and regular travelers to Mexico came with water and then used what I provided. They were the thankful guests, not the expectant ones. I left a full bottle for "big water drinkers" on Monday, though they did not return until that evening. When I went downstairs the next morning the empty bottle was on the table. Wow! "Big water drinkers" was an understatement. This was the most anyone ever used. It was filled, again, that day.

What I will never understand is why I did not buy a second large bottle for the guests so they would have two to start with. In fact, even the idea of doing so never crossed my mind. It was over dinner after I stopped being an Airbnb host in Mexico that my sister and I were talking about Baja. Somehow the issue of potable water in that house came up. It was only then that she said I should have had two large bottles so I would not have been fetching water so often. I wish this idea would have surfaced when it mattered. We both laughed. Amazing how obvious solutions can be so elusive.

When it came to food staples, the house had even fewer offerings than it did pots and pans. The big fridge had limited condiments guests could use. In the cupboard were spices, oil, and items prior guests left behind like tea, honey, and canned tuna. Usually there was butter, oil, salt, garlic, and hot sauce. Guests provided spices, vinegar, tea, honey, cooking spray and assorted items that I left in the cupboard for everyone. Most of the basics were duplicates of what I had or something I would never use. The two cans of tuna went to a neighbor's dog. Even without a major grocery store, Todos Santos had much more than the essentials one needs to cook with. Several guests cooked fresh fish. Some nights I could smell what was for dinner. Even not eating meat, I was jealous of the aroma as I reheated leftovers in the microwave.

A day or two before guests arrived, I was busy cooking several meals to freeze. Three individual servings were about all that could fit in the tiny freezer of the dorm-size refrigerator I had upstairs. I would let other meals thaw in the fridge, reheating them when I got hungry. Feasting off a large green salad for days, making egg salad, and blending fruit for smoothies also sustained me. I tended to dine on some version of reheated roasted vegetables each Airbnb visit, a versatile meal that can be eaten on its own, rolled in a tortilla, put over rice, quinoa, or pasta, even mixed in with eggs. Scrambled eggs, sweet potatoes, and baked potatoes were about all the actual cooking action the microwave would see. It really was remarkable how well and healthy I could eat with what I considered minimal amenities.

During a conversation with a couple who rented the house something came out about what I eat, so I explained my routine of cooking, freezing, reheating. I mentioned they probably saw I had left some food in the freezer because I did not need to eat that much during their stay, nor did I have the room for it upstairs. They looked at each other and then at me. She said she thinks they may have eaten my pesto. It was funny how she said it, as though there was my pesto and pesto for guests. Sorry lady, there was only mine. I took a deep breath, acting like it was no big deal. In the big scheme of things, it was not worth getting upset over or making even a mild stink about. They said they enjoyed it and offered to replace it. I said no need to. Considering pesto is what originally came in the jar it was easy to mistake it for store bought. Something made the guests rationalize they were allowed to consume it even though all my food was together in one section of the large downstairs freezer. With most items being in plastic reusable containers, it was obvious it was not store-bought food. That was a lot of pesto for four people. I suppose I was lucky more of my food did not disappear because of them or others.

Initially, I hauled the microwave, containers of prepared food, spices, pantry items, and everything in the fridge up and down the stairs in between guests. This quickly got old and cumbersome. Not having a fully stocked kitchen, whether it was the full-sized one or the makeshift one upstairs, was the best solution. I did not want guests to eat my food in the refrigerator or cupboards, so tempting them was not smart. I also did not want the upstairs closet to smell like food because all of my clothes were in there. It was not an ideal way to live, but it worked.

In Tahoe the experience was completely different. People did not have access to the kitchen other than to keep things in the freezer or refrigerator, or to heat things up in the microwave. Their limited access did not allow them to know if it was a well-equipped kitchen, unless they snooped around when I was not looking. I never noticed food going missing. If they used condiments, no big deal. However, just because people were not supposed to use the Tahoe kitchen did not mean they followed the rules. One morning I got up to eggs and ham being cooked. My expression said plenty. I explained the house rules say no cooking. They said, "Really?" "Yes," I replied. I told them to enjoy their meal, but from here on out the microwave was their cooking apparatus. Part of my review to them said: "They came intending to cook breakfast even though the listing says no kitchen privileges. It worked out fine—except for a spatula handle was melted a bit."

Silverware was used, sometimes a bowl or plates, even a glass or two. I did not have that many expensive things, but people seemed to gravitate to them, especially the large Riedel wine glasses. They were on a top shelf, with cheaper ones easier to grab. But they were the prettier, more interesting looking ones. The only stipulation was they were not to take glassware into the hot tub. I had plenty of plastic glasses for that activity. While Riedel's website says it is fine to put the glasses in the dishwasher, I never did. But how were guests to know this? I was concerned they would fall over in the dishwasher, or someone would try to squeeze too much into it and the glasses would clank together and break. It has always been rare when I would put stemmed wine glasses in a dishwasher, so I was constantly taking them out and washing the guests' glasses by hand. I was even wary of guests hand washing them.

The block of Henckels knives was the other nice thing in the Tahoe kitchen. I also found them in the dishwasher. This dulls the blade and shortens the lifespan of the knife. Again, I went about hand washing them. Once I was "caught" by a guest washing the knife they had used. They were so apologetic I started to feel bad I did not leave it there until they were gone. I explained how I use the knives all the time, so I did not put them in the dishwasher and I added how hand washing keeps them sharper. All of this made me realize I was never going to be able to put in the house rules every little quirk of mine I wanted someone to accommodate during their stay. Deep breaths and understanding were going to be required on my part.

## Feed Me

It did not take long for me to become disappointed if no food was left for me after people stayed at the Baja house. Guests spoiled me. Until food started showing up in the refrigerator, on the counter and in cupboards I would have never imagined I would eat other people's food. Almost everyone in Todos Santos cooked something at the house, even if it was only breakfast. One duo ate in almost every night. The propane dropped dramatically after their ten-day stay. Often, I did not need to go to the grocery store for a few days after Airbnb'ers had been at the house. It made sense. These people could not take food with them. Many were leaving my place headed for the airport in San Jose del Cabo. Security and customs would not allow most of what they left behind—bottles and produce. I doubt people would have wanted to haul it with them even if it were permissible. Even those who were going to other destinations in Baja usually did not have a cooler, so preserving perishables was not possible. In the hot, humid desert food does not last as long it does in more temperate climates. Instead of putting sugar and flour in canisters on a shelf as I have done every other place I have lived, in Mexico they were stored in the refrigerator. Rice and quinoa were in sealable containers, not necessarily what they came in.

Containers of leftovers got tossed without looking at what was inside. I was willing to consume whole fruit and vegetables left behind, but not half eaten food. It made me wonder if people were too lazy to toss it, or maybe they would have felt guilty for doing so, or perhaps they thought someone would want their used food. I do not know what a professional maid would do with food like this, or any edibles. I was the maid and did what made sense to me. Eating other people's food might sound icky, but why throw away perfectly good produce? It was not like I was consuming a half-eaten sandwich or restaurant leftovers. It was whole tomatoes, half a watermelon, a lot of limes, and liquor. Eggs, rice, salsa, granola, chips, crackers, beans—all were left behind. Some opened, some not. Some I ate, some I tossed. More than once I had enough ingredients for a yummy salad, with dressing courtesy of the same people.

The foodie who cooked for me left behind containers from Flora Farms in San Jose del Cabo, an organic restaurant a little more than an hour away. I had only heard good things about this place, though was disappointed when I finally went. There is a grocery there as well. This is where the jar of granola came from as well as a mango salsa. Neither went to waste.

One group left an opened sixteen-ounce jar of kosher dill pickles. A total gringo purchase. All the writing on the jar was in English. Cost was about $6. I enjoyed them, especially because I would never spend that kind of money on pickles. As more ex-pats call Todos Santos home and tourists come for a visit, local markets have stocked more non-traditional Mexican food items on the shelves. Some is imported from the United States, while so much comes from mainland Mexico. This is why goods cost so much more in Baja than mainland Mexico. Very little is made in Baja. Produce is the exception. So much is grown locally, but not everything.

Another group left a nearly full jar of parmesan cheese. This at least had the writing in Spanish. Cost, though, was nearly $14. Again, something I would not spend my money on. I enjoyed it, though.

Unopened bottles of wine did not stay that way for long. Some ended up going to dinner parties without anyone knowing it had been regifted. The good beer went upstairs. Same with the partial bottle of vodka. Cans of Tecate and Pacifico Light were another story. Often, I left those in the fridge for future guests, including the dog sitter.

Rarely did people leave food behind in Lake Tahoe. Most guests drove there from their home. This meant whatever edibles they had they could take with them. People came with groceries even though they could not really cook per my house rules. Many brought something simple for breakfast like fruit, cereal, yogurt. Skiers were apt to have fixings for sandwiches they could take to the slopes. Eggs were about the extent of the food I allowed to be cooked, and only because people were already in the process of doing so. After all, the stove was supposed to be off limits. One twosome bought a six-pack of drumstick ice cream cones. I could probably go the rest of my life without another.

## Making Friends

Becoming friends with Airbnb guests was not something I had much interest in until Mary and Jay arrived. They were staying at my place with their nephew while waiting to close escrow on their home in Todos Santos. This provided an instant kinship. They were not there on vacation, which put them in a completely different mindset. They were interesting in ways other guests were not simply because our conversations had more to do with real life and not about what activities to do for the next few days, though it was one of their main sports that convinced them to buy property in Todos Santos. I immediately knew these two were big into mountain biking when I saw the IMBA (International Mountain Biking Association) bumper sticker on their van. They loved discovering an Over the Edge bike shop was in town. This is where I rented a bike the couple of times I went riding in the area. Trails were being created all the time by the local shop owner and cycling enthusiasts. Once I discovered some of the trails, I regretted that my bike did not make the cut of things to bring south those first two winters as an Airbnb host. It took the third trip to figure out how to secure my mountain bike to the top of the rack I bought purposefully for my trip to Mexico. The carrier that fit into my hitch took the place of my bike rack when I realized everything I wanted to bring with me was not going to fit inside my Jeep Wrangler. Not knowing the cycling opportunities before that first trip south made it easier to leave the two wheels behind. Even if I had a bike to ride, Mary and Jay were at

114

a skill level I would not be able to keep up with, despite the fact I was at least a decade younger.

On their second night, the four of us were on the upper deck taking in the last remnants of the sunset. They popped a bottle of bubbly in anticipation of closing on their house the next day. They are travelers, having traded in a boat for this house in Baja. The crystal glasses we drank from came from London; packaged perfectly in a compact box for their former life on the water. It shows how you do not have to skimp even when you lead a no-madic lifestyle. Sharing a bit of Baja with them was wonderful. Hearing about their life interested me. This was such a departure from most guests whom I did not really care about. It is hard to care about guests long term when they stay a few days and at most you share a few hours with them. The fact that I remem-bered Mary and Jay's names was huge; that is not something I usually did. I had gone a whole week and did not know some people's names even when our rooms were only a few feet apart in Lake Tahoe.

Jay scored points from the get-go when he found a centi-pede crawling near the laundry bin in their bathroom. Ironically, that next day I had a blog post about my experience sleeping with one of those multi-legged critters. For peace of mind, I chose to believe it was the same centipede. I did not want to think about there being two or even more of these stealth crea-tures living inside with me and my guests. Jay captured it, then released it down the road a bit. They are great animals in the wild because they eat bad critters like cockroaches. But inside, they are totally unwelcome, at least by me even if they were to nosh on the random cockroach in the house.

The centipede I found woke me up in the middle of the night. It must have been in my hair for me to hear it. I leaped across the dog to get out of bed, turned on the light and saw the six-inch hairy thing inching along parallel to AJ, who remained oblivious to all of this. I grabbed the glass off the nightstand with the intent of trapping the slithering thing. Instead, I dumped water on the bed. The centipede was nowhere to be seen, having presumably scampered under the bed. The dog just looked at me wondering what the heck I was doing at that hour. It is just as well she never knew she was sharing the bed with another being besides me. I cannot imagine what would have happened if she tried to paw at it or wanted to see how it tasted. AJ and I slept downstairs that night. If Airbnb'ers had been there, I might have asked to come in. More likely I would have had a fitful night in the Jeep.

Andy, my neighbor, helped me search for the centipede the next day to no avail. He told me about the centipede in his closet from a month earlier and how he tossed it in haste toward my yard. It was amazing how easily I convinced myself his centipede and mine were the same one. Otherwise, it would mean there were potentially three of these creepy crawlers in close proximity. I refused to do any research about centipedes regarding how many might live together, how likely they were to return to a physical structure, or where they like to live indoors. I knew I was lucky neither AJ nor I was bitten. That would have been painful for me, and I do not want to know the trauma it would have caused a geriatric canine who weighed much less than me.

After Mary and Jay got settled in their new house, I visited them. What a stunning view of the desert and mountains. Perfect for enjoying a margarita, which they made from scratch. It is one of those things you learn to do while in Mexico, mix a margarita. The difference between their margarita and what my sister taught me was the simple syrup. My sister dissolves sugar in water on the stove for the syrup, which is then stored in the refrigerator to be ready at all times. Ice, tequila, fresh squeezed lime juice, and orange liqueur are all that are needed, maybe a splash of club soda. I am spoiled now. Margaritas in Mexico really do taste better than what is served in the United States. A year later I found out about the Mexican liqueur Damiana. It is sweet, but also somewhat earthy. Now my margaritas are topped off with a shot of it.

As for Mary and Jay, they were walking distance to one of the best Italian restaurants in town. This is where we dined the first night as friends. No longer were we host and guests. Other times we would meet for breakfast before one of the community meetings in town. They immediately got involved in the town, going to events (some we did together like the biennial home tour), frequenting stores, getting to know people, and volunteering as an English teacher even though math was Mary's background. With their gardener, they started a shared mulching program with his other clients so they would have organic material for their yards. When they were guests, I told them about the movie "Patrimonio", which they watched while they were at my place. All of this showed me they were homeowners who cared about the environment and the town they would call home part of the year.

They pitched stories to me for my website and the *Gringo Gazette*, a publication in Cabo San Lucas that I freelanced for. They also scratched their heads as to why my sister and brother-in-law's house was not selling. They raved about the craftsmanship, the layout and location. The lack of buyer remained a mystery to all of us.

That spring of 2020 I left for the States before they headed to their main home on the East Coast. It can be normal for part-timers to not stay in great contact with all their friends from their second home. It is like you are friends in the moment, with what you have in common being what you do together in that location. That is not to say all my friendships from Baja were like that. Some are lifetime friends who I have regular contact with. Others, though, they are strictly Baja friends. Mary and I had sporadic contact while we were not in Baja at the same time, but then things faded as my time there as a part-time resident ended.

Sleeping wih Strangers

# CHAPTER THREE

# Don't Come Back

## Broken Rules

With guests cuddled up on the couch, the living room had been taken over. Not what I wanted to see. I never got used to my own house not being welcoming to me. My irritation quickly switched to anger as my eyes flashed on the wood stove. The handle was not locked. Crap. No doubt a stronger word was on the tip of my tongue. I had to consciously restrain myself from delivering a verbal lashing. I turned the light on in the kitchen, not caring that I had killed the mood in the adjacent room. I was pissed and they were going to know it. The online listing said guests absolutely may not use the wood stove. For those who do not actually read everything, the "do not use the wood stove" policy was also in the book in their room. Of course, that also meant they had to read. I used the stove too often to put a locking mechanism on it when I was not in the house. At least that was my rationale before this encounter.

No one who stays at an Airbnb rental can legitimately say they did not know about a certain rule. When every Airbnb guest pushes the final button to book a place, he or she has agreed to all the house rules. This is for all guests, not just the person doing the actual booking. Obviously, plenty of people do not read everything, but if something goes sideways, the online house rules will be the first line of defense for a host. Therefore, when I book a place, I share the listing with those I am traveling with so they can read the rules. My rules ran the gamut from no smoking to no parties to not using bath towels at the beach to no glass in the hot tub area.

Young and dumb. I ended up with a few of those types. This one went from trying to impress the girl to being made a fool of by someone who was probably old enough to be his mother. Again, I did not care. My house mattered more to me than his ego or this romantic interlude. Why they were even in the living room and not in the bedroom if they were going to be all over each other was beyond me. I would think a king-size bed would be more comfortable than any couch. They knew I was going to return at some point, so the mood was going to be broken no matter what.

I latched the wood stove door while asking why it was unlocked. I was stern, clearly upset, but not yelling or using any colorful words. Silence from the couch. I kept the door in the locked position whether there was a fire going or not. He clearly did not know it was not locked. Neither one would look at me. "I thought it would be easy," he stammered, trying to explain why he tried to start a fire in the first place. I had the no fire rule for this very reason. So many people neither know how to operate a wood stove, nor do they have respect for fire. Starting a fire in a device like this is easy if you know what you are doing. I deliberately chose not to ridicule him further by saying as much. The stove being off limits had everything to do with safety. The unintended consequences clearly could have been a house reduced to ashes. What if he had started the fire, but left the door unlatched and embers ignited the carpet and everything else? Maybe they could have put it out quickly, but what if they had gone to the bedroom and then the house fire started? The various scenarios that went through my head had me reeling. I did not care how much insurance Airbnb provided. I never wanted to test it. I loved that house and all my stuff. Ask anyone who has gone through a fire; it is more than just things. They are your things with so many emotions attached to them. Even worse, though, would have been if anyone were hurt because of such carelessness with the wood stove. I do not even want to think about whether they would have had the sense to make sure AJ was out of the house in the event the house caught fire.

He never said he was sorry, which pissed me off even more. She never said a word. I made sure my irritation was known by leaving the lights on in the kitchen, being purposefully noisy as I went about my business, and then all but slamming my bedroom door. Without apologies, it was a mild tantrum. For once, the review from them was not on my mind. Letting him know he had crossed a line was all that mattered.

I never did put a lock on the wood stove. I either got lucky or better guests booked.

## Dress Appropriately

While walking down the hall in shorts and a T-shirt in the middle of winter, the dude told me how the bedroom was cold. I was cold just looking at him. Multiple layers of long-sleeve shirts combined with long pants and socks were the norm for me in winter in Tahoe—and that was inside. I never wanted it so warm indoors that I would be comfortable with skin other than my hands, face and neck showing. The average temperatures in South Lake Tahoe in winter are forties during the day and twenties at night. The city, which is at an elevation of 6,200 feet, averages more than one-hundred-forty inches of snow in a season. It might be normal to be in shorts and short sleeves wherever this guy called home, but it is not the typical way to dress in winter living in the mountains.

Being new to the Airbnb hosting gig I thought I should be accommodating. Even so, this was not the first time to be irritated by what I considered an inappropriately dressed guest. I was still hung up on reviews being the lifeline to being successful and presumed at that moment this would mean adjusting to the needs of guests. Reluctantly, the heat went up. Why I did not listen to my gut is beyond me. My inner voice said not to give in and to heck with the review. She lost that battle, but eventually won the temperature war.

Sixty-eight was the customary setting for the furnace during the day no matter who was in the house. When paid guests were in the house, the overnight setting was sixty degrees. All of the bedrooms were uncomfortably warm when the heat was up and the doors were shut. If only I had told him to go back in the room, close the door and soon he would be comfortable in his summer attire. In retrospect, there were a lot better ways to handle this than to just roll over. Simply saying put on more clothes would have been warranted. Explaining how I do not heat the house to accommodate someone wearing so little clothing could have been another option. Doing things solely for money, which essentially is what kowtowing for a review is, should never be the starting point. It should only be one factor in the big picture.

Often in winter the house was much warmer than sixty-eight degrees because of the wood stove. At times it got so balmy with the fire that I wore short sleeves, thus looking like the unwanted guest. On rare occasions the back door had to be opened to cool off the house even though I strived to have the wood stove under better control, so I was not heating the outdoors. Prior to this guy I had guests ask for the heat to be turned up, which was understandable to a point. The furnace was normally off when the wood stove was going. Guests were in the back bedroom, which was the last place the heat from the wood stove would reach. Being uncomfortably cold is never a good feeling, especially when you are paying to stay someplace. It took a few encounters with chilled, short-sleeve wearing guests to figure out how and where to establish boundaries.

Even though the thermostat said it was seventy in the house when rude dude complained, I did not question that it was cooler in his room. After turning the heat up to seventy-two, I started sweating with a sweatshirt on. It was the first weekend in December; with these being the first skiers of the season. It was definitely cold outside, so I understood wanting it warm inside. Why this skinny guy did not wear more clothes baffled me. The entitled twit bugged me the entire time he was there. Arrogant. Selfish. Full of himself. You get the idea. Luckily, he was not the norm, but I did not know that at the time. I would guess he was in his early twenties. Airbnb mandates a person be at least eighteen to book a room. Too bad there was not a way to measure maturity level to have that be part of the criteria. There was no hiding that we did not like each other.

A down comforter was in the closet in his room. The book in the room encouraged guests to use it. Peaking in when the door was open proved the down comforter was not on the bed. Come on, I thought, at least use the bedding provided and dress reasonably before the thermostat goes up. Others used the comforter, so I know people were reading the book. Or maybe they merely assumed with it being in the closet it was fair game. I wondered who paid this guy's heating bill. Parents probably. He portrayed himself as a spoiled, overindulged boy who was used to ordering people around to get what he wanted. I felt like the hired help in my own home the way he addressed me, dismissing me like I was there to cater to him. Even though I was providing a service, I did not deserve to be treated so rudely. Being a journalist already made me jaded about people. Living with strangers made me like people even less.

I vowed not to give up control again. Reviews were not worth this awkward feeling in my home. In the blink of a weekend, I went from being willing to bend over, to determined not to do anything I would not let a friend or family member get away with. This was my home. I needed to find a reasonable, firm voice and set the rules as well as enforce them. Had this guest been cold and dressed appropriately by most people's standards, that would have been a whole different scenario. Then I would have gladly upped the temp to make a paying or non-paying guest feel comfortable.

The two other memorable chilled guys ended up being great guests. When I first got the booking, the guy said he would be bringing a friend. I wrongly assumed the friend would be female. I can only imagine what my expression was in the morning when I met the two men. They were friends, nothing more; not that I would have cared if they were a couple. What shocked me is they were sharing a bed as friends. They could not be from the U.S. Most guys in the States will not share a bed with another man for fear people will think they are gay. At least that has been my limited experience. Based on accents, I guessed one guest was Middle Eastern and the other Eastern European. They were probably in their late twenties or early thirties.

I spent about an hour chatting with the guy who booked the room, mostly about our respective jobs. I realized I did not spend much time talking to men outside of a work situation. This interaction was a nice change. The whole dynamic in the house was different with them being friends instead of a couple. I no longer felt like a guest in my own house. It was liberating to have the bedroom door open as I worked. I suppose I felt more comfortable doing so because their door was open. I also knew I did not have to shut out any uncomfortable romantic sounds. It was not uncommon that one guy was in the bedroom on his tablet, while the other was at the kitchen table on his laptop. They were the first guests to stay with the new doors finally in. Even though I was relieved to no longer have to explain the hole, I worried about them getting dinged. I needed to breathe. Deep breaths served me well for a lot of Airbnb-related stressors. Not only were the bedroom doors new, but the bathroom doors and all the closet doors were new as well. They were also the first to sleep on the new bedding. Had I known it would be two men staying together I would have left on the thinner, cotton sheets that I used in summer instead of having made the bed with flannel sheets. Just guessing their body temperatures were warmer compared to women's. But, then again, it was guys who were cold, at least out of bed.

## Difficult Children

Airbnb allows hosts to have some latitude when it comes to children as guests. Not every space would be safe for kids. With the hot tub and wood stove at the Tahoe house, these could have been dangerous for youngsters. Touching the hot glass would burn anyone. More than once embers popped out when I opened the wood stove. This could be horrific if a child were nearby. After all, I am pretty sure some guests were refueling the wood stove. Neither of my host locations was childproof, nor did I intend to make either one so. My sister and brother-in-law agreed children would be banned from the Mexico house, too.

On the listings were sections titled Policies as well as House Rules. Hosts were to check off various items that pertained to their property. This then allowed guests to filter searches to best suit their needs and desires. It also gave guests an idea of what to expect. On both listings "Not safe or suitable for children (0-12)" and "pets - Dog on property" were checked. The Airbnb portal says, "Children can travel on Airbnb, but some hosts have specified that their space may not be safe or suitable for children or infants. Infants [children under 2 years old] aren't counted as guests when you're booking a reservation and don't incur any extra costs. Some hosts count children as guests, which can add an additional guest fee to the reservation."

Not having kids of my own probably made me less tolerant when it came to the possibility of children as guests. I did not want them around at either location. I lived a pretty tranquil life, and they usually are disruptive in some manner. That really was not going to be tolerable in Tahoe because of working from home. Other than occasionally turning music up to hear it outside, my homes have always been fairly quiet inside and out. I tended to attract guests who for the most part were quiet as well. On reviews I often commented how quiet people were. This was great for me and the neighbors. Kids can be loud, cry, and can be destructive. I did not want any part of that. Plus, AJ, my aging dog, had never been around that many youngsters, so I did not want to put her in that position.

Even though I had the no-child policy, I let a man convince me his twelve-year-old daughter and nine-year-old son were responsible, and the bonus was he said they loved dogs. I surmised they were a blended family based on flight documents they left behind. I have no idea what the sleeping arrangements were. That aspect of the booking never crossed my mind until they left. Whatever the scenario was would probably be worthy of another story. Maybe it is no big deal for a brother and sister (step or otherwise) to share a bed at those ages. I know the boy was in the smaller bedroom because it was below my room. Door slamming and crying, and even swearing by him revealed where he was staying. All the outbursts were exactly what I did not want and proved why the policy was in place. So much for sticking to my guns and trusting my gut. I could not believe how this brat spoke to his dad. The tone, the venom. I would hate to see what he evolved into as a teenager and beyond. I had such a strict upbringing that outwardly disagreeing with my parents was not allowed, let alone yelling at them. There were always repercussions for slamming a door. Vacation as I knew it would have been over and a spanking to remember would have been my souvenir. It sounded like the kid got his way. The dad did not raise his voice. It sounded like he was trying to reason with his son. From what I could hear this style of parenting was not working.

At the start of their vacation, the parents and this nine-year-old came upstairs to check out the view, which I always encouraged. The sunsets were stunning, especially going a little higher via the spiral staircase. As the three adults chatted, AJ and the boy were a couple steps behind us. I heard AJ snarl and nothing more. That was all I needed to hear. She had not been aggressive with anyone in years, especially unprovoked. What did this brat do? She seldom made a sound except for snoring, so this unfamiliar

127

noise from her immediately got my attention. In Tahoe she would bark because a bear or raccoon was outside. In Mexico it was as though she had lost her vocal cords. That is why I wondered what the heck the kid had done. It had to be something significant to get a reaction out of the dog. After all, it is never your "kid" who instigates things, so it had to be the boy's doing. And while AJ had a persnickety streak, it seemed to be in the past. The kid's parents did not seem fazed. Maybe they are used to dogs snarling when their kids were around. Maybe they do not pay attention to what their kids do. I knew something was up, I just did not know what. AJ could not tell me, and the kid was not going to confess. I kept them from each other the rest of the visit because I was fearful AJ might have some negative association with him. I did not trust the kid, and I am sure he knew it. These two would be the last kids—period. This was AJ's yard, not theirs. I hated having to keep her inside.

I tried not to let my irritation with the family take hold. It was the holiday season after all. I messaged them about some kid-friendly Christmas events they might be interested in. This was well received, so perhaps I was a better actress than I thought. The girl and mom barely made an audible peep the entire time. I wonder if this was the norm for them or if they were trying to be quiet so as not to add to the chaos of father-son. When I found the air freshener on the shelf in the parents' bedroom, I knew this foursome was even more weird than I had thought. I still wonder what that was about. AJ and I were overjoyed to have this family of four leave. Neither she nor I wanted to be bothered by children or difficult adults again.

The difficult adult part, well, that I never had control over. However, from then on, no kids were allowed, just like the listing said. People still sent requests, like this one, "Hi Kathryn, just wanted to check in about the possibility of our son staying there with us. He is a super mellow 9-year-old. It would be my husband and I and my (Website hidden by Airbnb) just the 3 of us. Are you open to having a mellow child stay there?"

No, was the short answer.

# Unwanted Before Arriving

It was never a good sign to be irritated by guests when their arrival was still weeks away. It was no surprise things only got worse when they showed up. I know this husband-wife duo with their fifteen- and eighteen-year-old sons would not book again, nor would I want them even at the higher rate over New Year's. Too bad Airbnb does not let hosts say no to children of all ages. While it would have been possible to cancel the reservation, there would have been repercussions from Airbnb, like losing my superhost status and the possibility of not filling that time slot. Too much was at stake for me and my sister to even broach the idea with her.

The mom emailed two weeks or so before their arrival saying she did not realize her kids would be sharing a queen bed. They are grown men and cannot do that, she told me. Really? We from the United States have such odd customs where boys and men refuse to share a bed. It made me flash back to when one of my sisters and I were taking our two nephews skiing and our brother-in-law said the young teens could not share a bed. I did not get it then. I doubt I ever will. For as long as I can remember I have shared a bed with one of my sisters when traveling. I still would. Same goes with my mom. I have slept in the same bed with friends. I know the not sharing a bed thing is not true of all guys because more than two shared my Tahoe king.

The woman asked whether the couch would be a suitable additional bed. It would be possible to sleep there, but I doubted it would be comfortable. The cushions at the time were beyond their lifespan and the ends of the frame were wood, so not easy, or comfortable to hang one's legs over. She asked about a blowup mattress. I lied, saying I did not have one. She asked about extra bedding. I lied again. I did not want to increase my laundry by fifty percent. Plus, with the house on the market, I refused to create a situation where someone would be living in the middle of the house for five days. If they did so without my help, that was one thing, but I was not going to instigate or condone that scenario. The woman asked what I was going to do. What? This was not my problem. A light fleece blanket in each bedroom could possibly be "extra" bedding, I told her. My sleeping bag remained my secret. I was not about to offer it.

Being difficult and unaccommodating came from a place of feeling scammed. I was not going to create a third bedroom because she was too cheap to reserve that type of listing to begin with. She knew this rental was an excellent price for four people, especially over a holiday, even with the inflated nightly rates. The listing was straight-forward with the description: two rooms, each with a queen bed. Airbnb makes it simple and not confusing to list what a host is providing. Airbnb in turn allows renters to set searches based on various criteria. Full house, rooms in a house, types of beds, and number of bathrooms were all filters she could have chosen.

Airbnb in 2022 added fifty-six "categories" to the equation for narrowing down the perfect dwelling. Airbnb said this addition was to allow people to choose by style, location, and nearby activities. Some of those categories included: islands, national parks, amazing pools, design, iconic cities, chef's kitchens.

Shared homes were also a category. This is what I had in Tahoe. Categories not in my vocabulary include ryokan (a traditional Japanese inn or small hotel) and Cycladic, like what is found in the Greek islands with whitewashed adobe with rounded corners and flat roofs. With all those choices, it would be even harder to not get what you wanted or for the lodging to be different than your expectations. Pictures on both of my listings accurately reflected what was offered. In Mexico, it was visually clear even on a cell phone that the beds in Mexico were not king size. I would put money on it that the difficult woman's sons would not have shared a king bed if it were available, so that really was not the issue.

I kept wishing they would cancel. Deep down I knew this would not happen based on my strict cancellation policy and all the money they would be out. If she were too cheap to rent a three-bedroom house, she was too frugal to throw away money by canceling. I dreaded meeting all of them in person. This was such a foreign feeling even though I was rarely super eager to meet anyone. No matter the guest or which listing, it became a disruption to my life. The whole Airbnb thing was about making money. My early romanticizing about meeting travelers, having interesting conversations, perhaps even living vicariously through them as they traveled did not last long. As I was initially contemplating the whole hosting gig, I reflected on my solo travels where at hostels or *pensions* I had met people from all over the world, learned about them, their culture, and the places we were seeing together. Some are friends to this day. I wanted to re-create this sense of wanderlust through others. This romanticism faded rather quickly. In Lake Tahoe I was working full time, which meant sometimes I could not give the interesting people much time. I always shared what to do, and where to go locally and beyond.

I was hospitable, and the reviews reflected it. I will never know if I missed out on meeting interesting people because eventually I opted to engage very little with people.

Airbnb added to the problems I had with this family of scammers. The troublesome foursome needed help making it to the house. They called from town on arrival day saying they were at the hotel down the street. There is no hotel down the street, so I had no idea where they were. I tried to give the mom directions, but she said she was on a borrowed phone and that she wanted me to meet her. Exasperated, I said fine. We exchanged vehicle descriptions and I found them at Hotel California in the center of Todos Santos. At the house she showed me my Airbnb listing. What the hell?—was my reaction. Airbnb had my address being in town. That was so incredibly wrong. Repeatedly I sincerely apologized. She had printed the locator map and address as provided by Airbnb in case there was no internet connection. That was a good idea for this location, but usually not a necessity. However, she did not print the detailed directions that were also on the site. She said she never saw them. She may not have seen them, but they were there. Location details pop up after a booking is made but are not available when people are perusing rentals.

I was on the phone with Airbnb as fast as I could to ask how the listing location got changed. The person could not tell me. I asked to talk to someone who did know. The tech division got back to me within the specified twenty-four-hour period. This person also could not explain why I could not change the map location without their assistance. When I first listed the property, I needed Airbnb to set the location because there is no street address. No numbers are how it works throughout Todos Santos. It was not an anomaly to this particular house. Some houses have names as a way to distinguish them, but that does not help with GPS.

Without a street number it always amazed me how the water department and electric company knew where to deliver the bills. They were stuck into the gate since there was no home mail delivery. Directions on the Airbnb site mentioned the color of the gate. The for-sale sign was an unmistakable landmark. If I were to be a host again at a house without an address, I would put in the GPS coordinates since that is how most everyone finds places these days. Even when written directions are provided, people want to rely on their electronic devices.

What never got explained to me by Airbnb is how the map got changed. This was such an incredible annoyance for me and the guests. They were in an area of town they did not expect to be. Nor did they want to be a mile from town. The sidewalks are not great for getting around, though it is doable. I completely understood their frustration. While the house itself was what they were looking for (except for that third bedroom), the location was far from it. Previous guests never said anything to me, so I am not sure how long the incorrect information had been on the listing. After this incident I found more detailed comments on the Airbnb listing, ones not available to the general public, about the house not being located where they expected. I could tell my overall review was downgraded because of this. I do not blame those people. I blame Airbnb. I asked more than one Airbnb employee to give the guests who were lost some compensation for their troubles, maybe a voucher toward their next Airbnb booking. Airbnb said that was not possible but they would call them. I do not know if they ever did. I am not sure it would have mattered to this foursome, but at least it would have proved I was not the one who messed up.

Conversations with these guests during their stay were tepid at best. We clearly did not like each other. This was a rare booking where I was counting down the hours until they left. One of the kids ended up sleeping on the couch on sheets they bought and left behind. The review was average, with personal comments to me about how I could improve things. My review of them was average, stating how noisy they were. The boys often went up the spiral staircase where the views are best. They are the only people who were ever loud enough that I could hear them. It sounded like they were jumping up and down. It was alarming, agitating, and another unwelcome intrusion into my world. It was a long five days for me and probably in some ways for them as well.

## Police Involvement

Clearly, there are people I would like to never encounter again as guests. Only once did I write a review saying someone would not be welcomed back. This was to alert future hosts. I contacted Airbnb before I even wrote my review. Airbnb has a platform to resolve guest-host issues. To my knowledge he never engaged them. Airbnb allows people to publicly explain their side when a review is less than ideal, or even to publicly thank people for something that was written. I have no way of knowing if he read the review. He did not leave me one. He was that type of person. I warranted a good review, so it would have been nice to have received it, even from this guy who left me wishing I had sage to cleanse the house.

Matt was a single guy in his early thirties from Southern California who booked the house for himself for two nights. He said he was coming to Todos Santos to work with his architect because they had just closed on property in Pescadero, the neighboring town. I did not ask who they were. Even in our advanced technological world, I know most building projects in Baja require an owner to be present at times. It goes beyond wanting to ensure things are being constructed as they desire so his reason to be in town seemed legitimate to me. I did not even question only one of the two being there in person. After all, my brother-in-law never came to Mexico for the eventual sale of his house.

From the get-go something about Matt made me uneasy. When a police chief in the United States validates your concerns, you know your fears are warranted. I shared the drama with my friend Jill the day after Matt left. She told me she had a bad feeling about him when I said he was coming. Although her intuition is generally spot-on, I have no idea what I would have done with that information had I known it ahead of time. Canceling a reservation because a friend has a premonition would be unique, but maybe not a first. I doubt Airbnb would have seen this as a legitimate reason that would allow me to not be penalized. My neighbor, Tim, said he got a weird vibe from the guest, like maybe he was sad or depressed. Connie and Andy, other neighbors, said they noticed the pattern of lights were a little strange for those two nights. They could not put their finger on what was out of sorts, but something.

Both nights I slept with the French doors closed and locked. I never did this when it was warm enough to sleep with just the screen doors locked. Something told me to be extra secure. The screen door lock was flimsy. It held the doors closed but was not much security. Plus, even a child could figure out how to push through a screen door, so a lock on it is not all that useful. Why I locked the main doors I still cannot say. The guy never said anything to me that was inappropriate, nor were his actions threatening. It was a vibe that he cast off that clearly unnerved several of us. This was the one time I wished AJ were more of a watchdog instead of a love sponge.

The day he left I went into the downstairs area to clean, as was my normal routine. The contents of his wallet were on the coffee table under the laminated information I provided to guests. It included his California identification, not a driver's license. Also in the pile were credit cards, an ATM card, medical card, contractor's card and more. What alarmed me the most was a woman's driver's license with a different last name than his and different address, though still in Southern California.

I took a photo of both IDs as well as a single picture of all of his belongings. Maybe I had been a journalist for too long or watched too many crime shows. I knew to collect some evidence. Unfortunately, my fingerprints were on everything. I hoped it was not going to matter, and that his prints could be found if need be. I should have known better than to touch what he left behind with my bare hands since I was suspicious of him.

He came to get the belongings after I messaged him. I did not let him in, but I also did not let anyone know what was going on. I could easily have had a friend or neighbor wait with me until he showed up. I had nothing to defend myself with. The pepper spray I carried on dog walks was upstairs, as was the air horn to alert neighbors I needed help. As nervous as I was about him, in hindsight I have no explanation for not protecting myself in some manner in case things went sideways when he returned. In our brief exchange when he came back, he mentioned he had duplicate identification in the vehicle so he would have been fine if he had gotten to the airport without everything he had left behind. That was odd. Who has duplicate IDs? Sure, he would have a passport to fly, but was that it? How he said "duplicate identification" made me suspect there was more to that statement. Maybe the other was his license. Maybe the identification had different names. Maybe my imagination was in overdrive. I am also sure it was the word "duplicate" that made me suspicious.

But who would willingly leave a credit card behind? That is such a hassle to replace and means days without the ability to charge. He probably had multiple credit cards somewhere as well. One would think the other cards he left behind were of importance as well since he had them with him. Did he want to leave the stuff behind or expect me to mail it to him? While it is easy for a hotel in the United States to ship a guest something they forgot, it was not as simple in Mexico. Well, it was as simple, it is just that it literally takes a minimum of two weeks for mail to get from one country to the other. So, if he had wanted his things mailed, it would have taken a while.

He neither seemed perturbed at himself for having to double back to the house, nor anxious about time being an issue. Nor was he remotely apologetic for any inconvenience all of this may have been to me. He was eerily calm, like he was faking his calmness. The reason for the documents on the table was that this was his hiding place for them, or so he said. That seemed absurd, though I suppose it would be a less obvious location than in an underwear drawer. It would be understandable to hide things if he were going out to the beach or did not want to carry everything in his wallet, but he had been at the house overnight and did not leave the premises until the morning when he packed up. Even if it were a hiding place, it did not explain why he left them behind. The fact he said the wallet contents were important enough to hide made it even more strange that he appeared ambivalent about coming to retrieve them, as opposed to relieved and thankful. His reasoning for leaving everything behind felt like I was being lied to.

Before his return I had canceled his access code to the house. There were times when this was the last part of the cleaning routine, while sometimes it did not happen until the next guests were about to arrive. Little good this action did since I let him walk up to the door. However, at the time I did not know I would be seeing him again because I had not yet found his belongings. Changing the code was a significant gesture to ensure he did not come back in without an invitation. Why I invited him back is still baffling. Had he wanted to harm me, all he had to do was knock me down on the concrete floor. I would have been out—perhaps for good. After all, according to his driver's license he is seven inches taller than me and forty pounds heavier.

Even more eerie was that as I was cleaning, I realized only one of the two chef's knives was in the wood block. This discovery was after he had come back to get the contents of his wallet. By now my imagination was in overdrive. Was there a missing woman? Is that why he was traveling with her driver's license? Is that why he had multiple forms of identification? I cannot prove he took the knife. I never did an inventory of kitchen items after guests left. But I would swear both knives were there when he arrived. With encouragement from a friend and my sister who owned the house, I let Airbnb know what was going on.

I wrote, "Matt, the guest who just checked out today, left all of the contents of his wallet here. Among the ID was a woman's driver's license—Melody Nancy Reed (no relation to me) from Santa Barbara. He was traveling alone. She has a different last name and different address than what was on his ID. He had a CA ID, not a driver's license. He came back to get everything after I messaged him. It has left me feeling weird/uncomfortable that he had this woman's ID. I thought I should tell someone. So that is why you are getting this message."

Two hours later Airbnb wrote, "Hi Kathryn. Thank you for reaching out to us. This is Adah from Airbnb's customer experience team and I hope that this message finds you well. Thank you for letting us know. I have asked one of our specialized team to check the details of your guest. We are great full (sic) to have you with Airbnb. I'll go ahead and close out our conversation. If you have any other questions, please feel free to reach back."

That was all I heard from Airbnb regarding this incident. No one from the "specialized team" reached out to me for more information or to say they cleared things up with the guest or that they investigated my concerns. This alarmed me. Fortunately, for them and me nothing bad materialized from this encounter. I hope Airbnb is not always this cavalier when it comes to a host's concerns.

As the day progressed, I could not shake that something was wrong. I knew getting the local law enforcement involved was not going to do any good. It is not a crime to make someone feel uncomfortable, and I had no proof he stole the knife. I am not even sure I could have described the knife or identified it. I opted to call the police chief in South Lake Tahoe, California, who I had dealt with for years when I was a journalist there. He said it was extremely odd for someone to travel with another person's identification. This was calming in a way because it confirmed I was not off base with my apprehensions. The chief said he would see if there were a missing person bulletin out or something worse involving the woman in question. It took a couple days before he got back to me because the woman was not at the address on her license. He was able to determine the two were boyfriend and girlfriend, and that she was very much alive. He could not answer other questions. To this day I still believe there is so much more to the story than I will ever know.

My journalistic instincts were not firing on all cylinders that day or long after because it was not until writing this book that a friend suggested I search online for the names on the two IDs.

Nothing much came up other than several years earlier on Facebook Matt put out a request asking friends if they had an old Verizon phone he could borrow for a couple days. A phone that perhaps cannot be tracked? My imagination was off and running again.

Matt no longer has an Airbnb account, at least not under the name he used when he stayed with me.

## Needy Guests

Being in the communications business my whole career one would think interacting with people would bring me enjoyment. I learned as an Airbnb host that there is such a thing as too much communication. When there was a lot of interaction with a guest before their arrival, I knew they would be even more needy in person. This was true at both locations. My attitude toward these types only got worse the longer I was a host. Good thing it is hard to detect tone through email. Of course, I wanted to make sure they had the best vacation possible, but as we know, even that simple idea was not always achievable when people booked a two-bedroom house when they needed three bedrooms. Giving suggestions for what to do was fun, but answering every little question got tiresome. It went beyond these people being curious, attentive to details, and super organized in advance. They were the types that did not want to leave anything to chance. Part of the fun of travel is self-discovery, figuring things out once on the ground, to not have every minute planned, and to be a bit free spirited.

"Hola again Kathryn, Just checking about grocery shopping for our stay. Would you recommend doing this after arriving at the airport? Is there a good supermarket en route? We prefer to buy produce organic and wonder if this is an option in Todo (sic) Santos? One more query, due to past back surgery, I need two pillows for sleeping and wonder if you have extra at the apartment?" That was his fifth correspondence with me. The questions were not unreasonable, but the barrage of messages was draining. I provided details about the numerous places to buy food and had the extra pillow on the bed upon arrival.

Maybe if I did not have other work to do all the endless questions from guests would have been less bothersome. Or maybe I am used to seeking out answers via friends and the internet. I wished these people would do the same and leave me alone. On the flip side, I realized it made sense to ask me whatever they wanted because I was their point of contact. It was the incessant questioning that became annoying. It is also not how I travel. I wing it more. I inquire about restaurants once I am at my location, but never have I asked about grocery stores. Unless there is some high-end restaurant that would need reservations, I do not worry about what and where I will eat. With people living everyplace I travel to, I know food and water will be available.

This was a Canadian couple coming down to celebrate their son's thirtieth birthday. They had so many questions ahead of time I wish I were getting paid by the hour based on time spent emailing them. The son was spending his second winter in Baja camping and surfing. The parents wanted to escape the cold. The plan was all three would stay at the house. Everyone who had been living in a vehicle in Baja considered the Mexico house to be luxury accommodations compared to camping. Merely having indoor plumbing was a welcome change for these travelers.

In that same email, which was via the Airbnb platform, he gave me a personal email address for reaching him going forward. I ignored it. I preferred to take Airbnb's recommendation to communicate solely through their site. This way the dialogue was recorded, so to speak, and was easy to reference by the company if either guest or host had an issue needing their attention. I kept interfacing via Airbnb until the couple started texting and stopped responding on Airbnb. They said the cost of using internet in Mexico was prohibitive. While I paid an outrageous amount of money for my cell phone, my plan with AT&T allowed me to call the United States from Mexico without an added fee. I could also call anywhere in Mexico, as well as call Mexico and Canada from the United States. For anyone calling me from the U.S. or Canada it was as if they were calling me in the United States. This was the best setup for working as a freelance writer while out of the country. People would never know I was in Mexico. Plus, it was perfect for keeping in touch with friends and family back in the U.S. I never had to think about the cost of texting, calling, or emailing. Even when traveling to Europe the most I have ever paid was $10 a day for internet access. While this can add up, especially if two people are on the same plan using separate phones, it is not an outlandish expense. I never knew what their fee would have been. I just chose to be judgmental.

The judgment continued after check in. I did not understand why they would use an apparatus in an unfamiliar house that they had no experience with at any point in their lives. The woman asked me about the *garbinator*. At least that is what I thought she called it. An internet search revealed she was saying *garburator*. That is what Canadians call a garbage disposal. I figured out what she meant when she described the sink and where waste goes. They did not have one so she did not know what could go down it. She asked if a banana peel would be ap-

142

propriate. My eyes got big and mouth fell open. I refrained from saying, "Are you nuts? Do I need to disable it? Should I put tape across the switch?" Instead, I said, "Absolutely not" in as neutral of a tone as possible. Then she asked about coffee grounds. Another "no," with some distinct exasperation. I was not going to explain how only a little bit of grounds should go down at a time because I knew all they would hear was yes without the fine details. They acted like the disposal was a means for composting, when in fact that is not what this mechanism is for at all.

I said only small food particles should go down the disposal, that it was not to be treated like a garbage can that ground up food. I added that the cold water should be on when doing so, and then left to run a bit after turning the switch off. Better yet, I added, if you are not sure, then throw the waste in the trash. They looked at me like this was not going to happen. At home they put most of their food scraps into a composter, so throwing away compostable items like banana peels and coffee grounds was foreign to them. They seemed giddy with the thought of a new gizmo to play with. I was scared they were not understanding the purpose of a disposal. I envisioned needing to call my sister to relay the disposal needed replacing. Repeatedly, I stressed this was not a composting device. Composting was not an option for them at my home in Mexico, so they were going to have to come to grips with tossing things in the garbage. I chose not to compost because I was only a temporary resident in Todos Santos, and I had no intention of planting a garden. Of course, the trees and plants in the yard probably would have benefitted from a soil amendment. My neighbors were into composting, so I knew it was possible to do so successfully. They used horse manure to help with nutrients, and then mixed in mulched Neem branches with the vegetable matter from their kitchen to create a compost they could use year-round.

I did not take the time to thoroughly explain to these Canadians how food waste ending up in a landfill was better than plugging up the septic system with material that did not belong there. With them being so environmentally conscientious, they may have been interested to know disposals are water wasters. Some reports say the amount of water used for a garbage disposal is like flushing a toilet—about one-and-one-half gallons. That is assuming it is a new toilet. Ones built before the early 1980s could use seven gallons. Considering water is precious in Baja, dumping food waste in the landfill could be seen as being more environmentally friendly than using a garbage disposal. Todos Santos on average gets about six inches of rain a year. Rain and storm runoff from the mountains fill the aquifer that supplies the town with its water.

This house, like many others in Todos Santos, had the gray water flow to plants outside. At my sister's place gray water came from the kitchen sink without the *garburator*, both bathroom sinks, both showers, and the washing machine. This helped save water when it came to landscaping. After my hosting stint ended, I learned there are soaps that are better than others to use when gray water is being repurposed. At the time I never gave any thought to the shampoo, dish soap or laundry detergent being good or bad for the plants. It was a bit disconcerting at times to see all the bubbles around a tree being watered from the washing machine, but the gardeners never said anything, and I never inquired as to the harm of the suds. I always wondered what would happen if food scraps or hair got caught in the pipes. Maybe it would be no different than a clog in another sewer line.

Despite my best efforts to convince the Canadians not to use the *garburator,* they did. Repeatedly. It made a rather loud, distinguishable grinding sound that reverberated to where I lived upstairs. I am glad I never knew what foods they shredded with that flick of a switch. Even happier it kept working after they left and no pipes were clogged on my watch.

The irritations, though, continued. These Canadians were the only people at either location to ask for a clean set of towels. This came after they had been at the Baja house four full days and five nights. During the nine nights they were there I used the same towel. Why they could not do the same was beyond me. I also was not showering every day and guessed they were. It is warm in Baja. Towels dry, so a wet towel should never have been the issue. I did not have any fight left in me, so new towels were provided without attitude. The evening was already crappy, having learned my just-released book about snowshoeing at Lake Tahoe had a typo on the back cover. Snowshoer was spelled wrong. At the time, I did not know this drastic error would be easily corrected in a timely manner. I just knew I was not up for arguing about towels. The irony is this couple prided themselves on being eco-friendly with their recycling, food waste, and garbage. What about water, you two? Doubling my laundry load was not environmentally-sound judgment. I told them where the extra towels were. Not even a thank you.

My patience was wearing thin with these Canadians. There seemed to be an issue with these people every day. Thank goodness we were not sharing a living space like in Tahoe. I might have needed to leave for part of their stay. Even though I do not want to see them again, they were extremely nice. Apparently, I am one of those rare people who will use the same towel repeatedly. Friends and family told me I was unreasonable to expect people to use one towel for a nine-day stay. Enough chastising from those I queried proved I should have been offering fresh towels to guests who stayed a week, maybe even for shorter bookings. My penchant for long towel use was reinforced during college because I did not want to do laundry often nor could I afford to. My towel changes today are random. I have come a long way from my childhood when I used a towel only once before it went in the laundry basket. That luxury stopped when California was hit with a significant drought. I have no memory of how many days my mom said to use the towel, but those wasteful days were never to return—not at my parents' nor in my own home. I do not recall when hotels started asking guests to hang up their towels to re-use them or put them on the floor for new ones. Airbnb hosts are not hotels. Hang the towel, it might be the only one you get, was my philosophy.

Naturally, the next booking was for thirteen days. I dreaded what another long stay might mean. Even though this delightful couple never asked for towels, I learned my lesson and took them fresh ones on day five. They only used one per person. Those were my kind of guests. This couple had been living in their vehicle for the past few months, so who knows when they had new towels while out on the road. While the towel issue was one good thing about these two, it was not all wonderful.

Based on how long it took me to scrub the grime from the bathtub, I would have preferred to have done more laundry had I been given the choice. The woman was verbally excited about the tub when I showed her around. I reminded her water is precious in Baja and said I would prefer she not soak in the tub. It was not just a ring on the enamel, it was filth from the water line down and all along the bottom of the tub. They may have washed clothes in

146

there since the washer and dryer were off-limits. But I think the people were that dirty because I never saw clothes outside drying, so it was hard to believe the gunk in the tub was from laundry. The first week was one couple, with two friends of theirs joining for the second week. The shower and tub are separate, so no one was having to stand on the floor of the dirty tub. Still, there is no way a tub could look like that after one soak. I never left a ring after one soaking. Maybe she was in there every night.

These were the people who came by to check out the house before actually booking it. Airbnb discourages hosts from doing this. Mostly the caution has to do with Airbnb not wanting people to book outside their portal. What could be more worrisome is if they were not really potential guests and instead were casing the place to see if there were something they wanted to steal. This did not cross my mind until I read about that possibility after the fact. I understood wanting to see a place before putting out money for it. Pictures can lie. I have been on the wrong side of that as a guest. In this case the couple said the house looked better than the pictures. I took that as a compliment even though I had taken the photos.

## Potential Buyers

In Mexico it was hard not to get a glimpse inside the rental space while guests were there because I had to walk by multiple windows to get to the front of the house where my Jeep was parked. Several board games, puzzles and cards were available for guests to enjoy. I smiled when all ages would be playing a game. Many remarked it added to their enjoyment and that it got them off their electronic devices. The eclectic bookshelf was another subject of conversations and comments in reviews. My analness had the books in alphabetical order by author so I always knew when someone had been perusing the reading material because books were no longer how I left them. I encouraged people to take any book they wanted and to leave something behind if they so desired. The selection was always changing. Both winters I drove to Todos Santos as a host I had brought a load of books with me from my storage unit that I had never read. It took a while, but I started each one. More than one ended up on the downstairs shelf without me finishing it. Maybe someone else would find it redeeming.

In Tahoe I rarely saw what the guests' room looked like because the door was usually shut. A few times when I could see in, I was surprised by the total chaos. I thought I could be bad when traveling. These people made me look like a neat freak. I do not know how they found anything. They had a dresser and closet to put their clothes in. Nope. The floor, not even their suitcase, seemed like a better choice.

When it came to messes in Mexico, it did not really matter until there was a house showing. Usually, I was given at least twenty-four hours' notice by the real estate agents that someone would be over with potential buyers. On the Airbnb listing I alerted potential guests the house was for sale. Providing this information was not a house rule in the traditional sense, but I had to make sure it was part of the Airbnb listing to avoid it being a surprise when people saw the for-sale sign on the gate as they drove in. More important, I did not want it to come as a surprise that they could be inconvenienced by house hunters. Comments and questions from the Airbnb'ers about the real estate sign clearly indicated they had not read every detail.

Real estate agents only came through a few times the first season. Traffic picked up quite a bit the following winter. The guests were never outwardly bothered by this, as they were usually away playing tourist for the day. Most said they would straighten things up. Peeking through the windows I could see if the house looked presentable. I was not sure what I was going to do if it were a total mess. What would their reaction be if I tidied up a bit?

One couple looked at the house without Airbnb guests staying the night. They liked it enough to come back a second time. This time it was filled with four people in their early thirties. These were the two who were staying for thirteen days, while their friends joined them for a week. They all became better known to me as the dirty bath tubbers. It never dawned on me I should check out the tub before the showing. I will never know what it looked like that day. Everything looked good when the original two guests straightened up for a different showing. Unbeknownst to them I had walked through the downstairs to make sure it was presentable. They were using their bedding; the house linens were in the closet. Since they had been living out of their vehicle, it was easy enough to grab what they wanted out of the truck. This probably freed up space for them in their vehicle. Their things looked nice, even better than what was provided. Maybe it was more comfortable as well. After a quick walk through, I had no reason to suspect things would not be fine for subsequent showings, so I did not bother to enter before the repeat clients arrived.

Boy was that a bad decision. I did not like the vague answer from the agent when I asked how it looked inside. I needed to see for myself. A mattress, presumably from the couple's truck (they had driven to Baja and had been camping), was in the living room with some of the house linens as though someone were sleeping there. That alone perplexed me because two couples were staying there. Maybe one was a snorer, or they were fighting. Boxes of crap from the truck were everywhere. They had needed to make room to haul their friends, so their belongings had to go somewhere. It was clutter, not dirt. It was not inviting. No wonder the offer on the house came with the stipulation all Airbnb rentals had to cease. What I was told is the potential buyers did not trust the guests to not damage the house, so they also wanted detailed pictures taken. If anything were amiss between the time of the offer and time of possession, my sister and her husband would be liable. A contract with those people was never signed. Just as well; it was a rude, lowball offer.

I did not share my thoughts with my sister that perhaps those Airbnb guests were part of the problem. I did not know how to fix the situation going forward. I felt a bit responsible for that deal not going through. This house had been on the market for years and was not selling for reasons I could not imagine. I decided it was time to be a bit more aggressive with guests. Never, though, did I ask to see the house before a showing. I thought that would be crossing a line and would make them uncomfortable because clearly I would be judging how they were living as it related to cleanliness and clutter. Somehow taking the more passive, and in many ways more intrusive, approach of going in without their knowledge seemed like a better idea. Plenty of people live in filth and chaos at home so they were not going to be any different somewhere else. They were on vacation, so being super tidy was not a priority either. And it simply was not their house to sell, so they had nothing to lose by not making it look immaculate.

For the next showing I went in the house without the guests' knowledge. Crap. It did not look at all how I would have it if I were them. Did the guy even tell his wife and adult son there was a showing? Or did he slough it off knowing they would not be there so the others did not need to know? Maybe no one but the guy even knew the house could be shown while they were there. I took the pot off the stove and put it in the dish drainer. I hoped it had only been used for boiling water. Chairs got pushed in, stools rearranged, pillows fluffed, and bedding adjusted. It was still far from perfect. I had crossed a line I never thought I would, which was to move things while the space was rented. I figured if guests ever asked why things had been moved, I would say the agent did it. The problem with this line of thinking is the guests returned home before the showing. They said they were going to have lunch and would be out before the potential buyers arrived. That answered the question about whether everyone knew what was going on. I would never know if the place looked worse than when I last saw it. I left the property before they finished their meal. They never said anything about things being moved. It was tough balancing being the landlord for my sister and wanting to do what I could to get the house sold, while also being the host to guests who expected privacy and for me not to enter their space.

Later the real estate agent said the Airbnb clutter had nothing to do with the lowball offer or the stipulation about ending short-term rentals. Still, I never again trusted guests to create a presentable environment. The house never went into escrow while I was an Airbnb host, but it did the following fall. Good thing I had not planned on a third season doing the Airbnb gig in Baja.

## Assorted Annoyances

As with any type of employment, there is always room for improvement in so many aspects and usually by all involved. But who is the boss and who is the employee in the world of short-term rentals? In this case, Airbnb is the boss because the company has the final say. After all, the company is providing the platform everyone is using. Some could argue this then makes hosts the employees and guests the customers. In the world of the customer is always right, that can be a hard reality to accept especially when Airbnb promotes hosts as being their own bosses. Some people may merely view Airbnb as the middleman because it is taker, keeper, and distributor of the money. Akin to a credit card company, Airbnb collects payment from customers and pays it out to hosts, aka business owners. I would venture to guess most hosts and guests have little or no interaction with those thousands of employees receiving an actual paycheck from Airbnb. This then relegates Airbnb to practically being inconsequential to hosts and guests outside of being a technological tool.

I viewed guests as clients, and Airbnb more like corporate headquarters as opposed to a direct boss. No one was checking in with me like a boss does. Plenty of emails came from Airbnb, but they were sent to all hosts. I was not special in their world, which may have had to do with the minuscule amount of revenue I generated for myself and them. Perhaps the company has more intimate relationships with the big money-makers.

In this digital age, consumers, be they housing guests or customers of some other sort, have more power today via reviews. It can be via Yelp, through a company's website, social media and certainly directly on Airbnb after a stay. With Airbnb, though, the reviewer is not anonymous. Airbnb makes it easy for the other person to counter a less than favorable review. Reviews are also an opportunity for people to make suggestions without ever confronting a host directly. On occasion guests left me private messages through the Airbnb portal. Other people told me in person what they thought. This could come across as intrusive and hurtful instead of being beneficial and welcome.

One couple was ready to remodel my South Lake Tahoe room. They thought the window should be turned into a door and went about telling me how to do this. Considering the king-size bed abutted that wall, they seemed unfazed the furniture would no longer fit. Nor did these remodelers consider what it would be like in winter with snow piling up. In big winters when the roof needed to be shoveled the bulk of the white stuff went in the area where "their" door would be. They talked about how much more money I could charge for something that was truly private. I smiled, or maybe I smirked. I tried not to sneer. I wanted to suggest they rent something different next time and not worry about my living arrangement. Had it been a comment in passing, that would have been one thing, but they went on and on, as though they had been consumed with this topic for the better part of their short getaway. I worried if I explained what living in snow country was like and that one day I envisioned the primary bedroom not being a rental, it could come across as ungrateful or challenging or some other negative adjective. What I was making off all guests was not covering as much of the mortgage as I had hoped, so it certainly was not creating reserves for remodeling. I am sure they were trying to be helpful, but I only heard condescending rudeness.

I wanted to suggest they read more carefully about the lodging they book so in the future they would not be surprised to learn they did not have a private entrance. I was shocked they were not the only ones thinking the Tahoe house was something it was never advertised to be. Hello? The listing said it was a room inside a house shared with the host. Airbnb's categories make it clear where a person will be staying. It also states what the shared spaces are. The site is not difficult to use or navigate. All descriptions are clear, so the guest knows exactly what to expect.

They were not the only ones to confound me. Those who left trash all about puzzled me. Of course, they knew someone was going to clean after they left (which was always me), but some people were utter slobs. Garbage at times was left in every room. No attempt was made to put waste in the provided cans. I wish I knew who left the tangerine peel on the upper roof behind the ledge where people would sit to get the best view of the sunset in Todos Santos. Perhaps I expected too much of people. But then again some of these people were the same ones who left the place in a state of disarray knowing the house was going to be shown to perspective buyers. Leaving trash like that, though, irritated me. It was bad enough to clean up after messes in expected places, but this was uncalled for. What if it had been something that would become rancid and took me longer to discover it? The used condom, well, that was the nastiest thing I came across. This was in Tahoe at the foot of the bed. Maybe it got thrown there when all the fun was over. At least they were being responsible, but the ick factor of finding it and then thinking about what was going on in my bed made my stomach turn.

I will never understand discarding trash anywhere but in an appropriate receptacle or flushing it if that were an option. This would be something like a tissue in Tahoe. I found them wadded up on the floor. (In Mexico all paper, including toilet paper, had to go in the garbage can because of the sewer/septic systems.) Saying an orange peel is organic is not a reason to leave it behind. That is not something a bird or rodent or insects would normally be eating. This mentality about garbage is why when I would go on a dog walk AJ's poop bag would do double duty as a trash bag. I am a firm believer in the hiking mantra that if you carry it in, you carry it out. Same concept goes for rooftop views. If you take it up the stairs, take it down the stairs. Same goes for condoms, use it and dispose of it.

I regret not saying something to the guys who smoked at the Mexico house, which was a complete violation of my house rules. They did so outside, but still it was wrong. Apparently, I was still having issues with boundaries and bad behavior even after my stint as a host in Tahoe. These two had been so helpful when the new refrigerator arrived that I let this cloud my judgment. Regrettably, I neither asked them to stop immediately, nor did I include their behavior in my review. One of the guys communicated fluently in Spanish with the delivery people—something I could not do. Both guests moved the old fridge out of the way without scratching the floor. Wrongly, their helpfulness and kindness outweighed the smoking, at least when it came time to being completely forthcoming on the review.

I mentioned smokers in a couple Tahoe reviews, so it is not like I was afraid of the subject matter. I wrote: "The only complaint is that in my 'house rules' I have that there is no smoking allowed anywhere and I saw them smoking out front. Only for that reason I would not want them back at my place, but otherwise I highly recommend them as guests." I had to change the rules in Tahoe to "anywhere" instead of only no smoking in the house because I saw people smoking out front. With wood chips a predominant part of my landscaping, the last thing I wanted was to have a guest start a fire with their cigarettes. Smoke also clings to clothing and hair, so the smell comes inside even when all the inhaling and exhaling are outside. I did not want the stench on furniture or linens either, or in any room of the house. This was my other smoking related review for a Tahoe guest: "While this would not be an issue for everyone, they are smokers. They did go out front to smoke, but I'm pretty sensitive to cigarette smoke and could smell it on them when they came in. Plus, they just flicked the ashes on the ground. I don't know where the butt went."

What later angered me even more in Mexico was finding empty cigarette packages on a high shelf in the large guest room. It was not a place I ever looked or bothered to dust. It used to have decorative décor, which I had relocated to the front room to make that area look more appealing. The only reason I saw the garbage was because I was standing on the bed to dust the ceiling fan. It could have been someone else's trash, but my gut said it belonged to the two known smokers. That is when I truly regretted not being honest in the review about them violating my house rules. A future host deserved to know about their behavior—the good and the bad.

While some people were oblivious to where trash should go, there were also the ones who did not understand personal space. My personal space to be precise. Try as I might to be polite, multiple Tahoe guests either did not understand or did not care that I was working in the room down the hall. After the pandemic that started in 2020, I am sure people better understand the concept of a host having a job that involves staying at home on a computer. These needy people made being an Airbnb host a job that interfered with my real job and my life. Even with the office or bedroom door closed, people would knock or talk loudly from the other side. What if I were not home? They would have to figure it out on their own. I wished they would always just figure it out because nothing was ever important. It did not help that I preferred working with the door open, so I did not feel like I was enclosed in a small box. I have never liked working with a closed door. I know this contributed to their belief I had an open door for them. Barging into the room was the worst. No gentle knock on the open door, or politely saying, "When you have a second, I need to ask you something." At least then I would not have been rattled and had my train of thought completely thrown off track. For those who write or are creative in some other way, where silence is serenity, such interruptions are beyond bothersome. When I took a break to get food from the kitchen, guests were apt to pounce on me for something. I am surprised I never slammed my office door or put a sign on it saying leave me alone, in a nice way, of course.

I would imagine with remote work now being the norm that many guests are working in their Airbnb units. Maybe some hosts are having to learn to be respectful of guests who need some quiet to make calls, interact with clients, and be on the computer without interruption. I know of only one guest in Mexico who was there for work. Everyone else was on vacation, even if they did some work while away from home. The working guest was employed by Colorado State University. CSU was part of a controversial project in Todos Santos, which included the boutique hotel that forever changed the waters where the fishermen launch their boats and return each afternoon with the catch of the day. It took all my restraint not to engage him in conversation about his employment. I did not trust myself not to say something potentially offensive. The last thing I wanted was to offend someone staying at my place.

Because I was living in tourist destinations guests acted like I was on vacation as well, with all the time in the world to chat. I never established a rigid line regarding my time because I wanted to be kind, helpful, and available. It was a balancing act to have the Airbnb obligation while also having a time-consuming job in Tahoe, writing books and blogs in Mexico, and trying to have fun in both locations. Being helpful was sincere. I wanted everyone to enjoy the town I was calling home. It was never just about the review, but people have no comprehension about the amount of my time they consumed.

My enthusiasm to engage with guests waned quickly in large part because of the type of visitors who were coming to Tahoe.

Most were from the greater San Francisco Bay Area, with many knowing the area they were visiting. They often did not want to interact with me anymore than I wanted to with them. The Bay Area is where I grew up, it is where I graduated from college, where I worked for several years, and lived before moving to Tahoe. I had neither the time nor the patience for their snobbery. As a rule, they had an attitude like they were better than me. It was as though these guests thought people living in the mountains were simple, uninformed, even uninteresting. This elitist stance was immediately off-putting. It was as though mountain folks were a different breed. Many could not believe I lived there year-round, thinking snow would be a reason to leave. The few people from the Bay Area who had little familiarity with Tahoe assumed in turn I knew little about San Francisco or its surrounding suburbs. They were the most surprised to learn I chose to leave all that behind and live in the mountains. This made me even more peculiar to them. Fortunately, that superiority complex was unique to people from that area. I never felt it from guests who lived in other parts of California, elsewhere in the United States, or in other countries.

I always asked guests where they were from because usually I had forgotten by the time they arrived. I rarely asked follow-up questions about their specific hometown in the Bay Area because I did not want to know more. The times I mentioned my connections to their part of California it suddenly seemed to bring more depth to me in their eyes. Until then they had me pegged as some flakey, uneducated, unsophisticated mountain woman. That type of woman may exist in Lake Tahoe, but she was not in my circle and certainly not the norm. Plenty of people were born in the local hospital, left for college, and came back to have well-paying jobs. Others like me fell in love with the mountains and found a way to have a career in Tahoe even when it meant reinventing themselves more than once in order to stay at the lake. I never had attitude about people from the Bay Area until I was a host. In many ways, the Bay Area still feels like home because it is where I grew up.

## Doing Laundry

I did not see their luggage, but even the smallest suitcase holds several outfits. When I heard the washing machine, I was perplexed so I casually asked if this was the start of their trip. "Yes" was their answer. So, on the second and third days you need to do laundry? I did not actually ask this, but I sure thought it. Bizarre. I have gone much longer than a week without doing laundry, whether I am at home or on the road.

Their behavior either proved not all in the group read the house rules or rules are for other people. They were not supposed to use the washer and dryer. My sister wanted to keep these old appliances operating as long as possible. The best way to do this was for me to be the only one using them. It also meant less water, electricity and propane being used. Plus, I did not want to provide detergent. It is doubtful guests ever realized a dryer in Todos Santos was a luxury. Most people, even gringos, line dry clothes throughout Baja. But here they were on day two of vacation with the washing machine chugging away. There was no getting away with using it without my knowledge unless I was not at home because the laundry area is right below the upstairs walk-in closet. The noise was unmistakable. I let it go. Interrupting the wash cycle was not going to solve the problem. I figured in a three-night stay that would be it. Nope. Wrong. They were back doing more laundry the next day. Maybe they could not mix their clothes to make one load. The travelers were a couple probably in their late thirties, with his mom and her sister. The mom was in her late seventies, with her sister a bit younger.

After that experience, I posted a note on the door saying, "Owner's Closet" and put string around the accordion doors so they could not be opened. Some guests opted to hand wash clothes; something I have done on my travels, so it came as no surprise to see items hanging outside either on the line or strewn about on the patio furniture. Finding lacy underwear and thongs spread on the outdoor furniture shocked me at first and then had me laughing. Those undergarments sure beat the cotton variety I wore. Mostly it was bathing suits and towels drying outside, along with the occasional wetsuit.

I did not want to tell them there was no guarantee there would be water every day, so it would be best to curtail unneeded and excessive use. Water was delivered most every morning to two eleven-hundred-liter tanks via a rickety pipe system that some described as looking like spaghetti. No mapping, no GPS, no GIS to know what really existed under that thin layer of dirt. In storms the pipes could become exposed. A neighbor once had to take the water company employees to various hardware stores in town to find the appropriate parts, often telling them what they needed to buy. He was never reimbursed for the supplies. It cost about $15; not much, but it is an illustration of how Mexico is a Third World country. There were times when the water deliveries did not come. Even though the threat of no water occurred with friends in the house, the tanks always stayed full when people who were paying were on the premises.

With the pipes not far underground, water leaks in the street were common. Once I found a tree suddenly growing in the middle of the road I was living on. It was a marker for the water company to know where the leak was. When a large, tire-swallowing hole opened on a main street in Todos Santos, a crate was placed over it. No reason to steal it, and it was obvious to steer around it. Workers get an A for creativity and improvising. In the United States when there is work to be done on a water line and potential disruption in service, the resident is notified days in advance assuming it is not an emergency. No notice in Todos Santos.

One time I did not know I was out of water until I heard gurgling and saw a trickle of water come out of the showerhead. The two water tanks were empty. If only the gardener had not come that day, there would be water. A neighbor discovered the valve for the line that lets water flow from the city line to the house tanks had been turned off. I did not know that valve existed until then. Another neighbor came to the rescue when he handed me his hose to start filling the tank; providing enough water for showers and toilet flushes for me and my friend who was visiting. I was still hesitant and waited on the shower. Despite being told it could take a couple days to fill the tanks, they were full the next morning.

With the town being located on the Pacific Coast, it gives the illusion of endless water even though the terrain is desert. Climate change is affecting Baja like it is elsewhere. The bulk of the annual six inches of rain comes in August and September, which is also prime hurricane season. While I never had to endure a hurricane, the house did. My sister and brother-in-law owned it when Hurricane Odile struck in 2014. Compared to so many other structures, theirs was not severely damaged. They did learn the hard way the chimney had not been built with rebar. Foliage on the plants and trees was ripped off, with only the trunks and limbs remaining.

## Interesting Pairings

I may have profited off illegal activity, though I will never know for sure. Clearly naive, at the onset I only envisioned couples, friends, and same-sex relatives would stay in a bed together. Instead, unique duos—and a trio for three long nights—came and went. I was not quite as open-minded and accepting as I thought I was. Apparently, some Puritan ideals had seeped into my subconscious that laid dormant until I became an Airbnb host. Still, I am not convinced all the arrangements were as the guests portrayed them to be. Most people volunteered information about their traveling companion even it was to merely state their relationship, like I am coming with my spouse, friend, or mother. Alarm bells never went off when nothing was mentioned. I learned the hard way I should have been asking more about the second person on the reservation. My hosting experiences changed my behavior as a guest. Now, without being asked, I volunteer who is traveling with me.

When a woman booked the Lake Tahoe room for a night the same day she would be arriving, it did not faze me. That had happened before without consequence. People often drive until they are tired and then seek shelter wherever they can find it. When I heard rustling outside, I went to see if the guests were having trouble getting the key out of the lock box. Before me stood a kid looking down at his tablet. He was ten, maybe eleven years old. Without pausing to look at me, he informed me his babysitter went to get something in the car. What? When the woman booked the reservation, she made no mention of traveling with a child. This felt so wrong, like I had been betrayed. I felt used before the two had even stepped inside. It was not going to matter her age. Female babysitter with preteen male had me seeing red flags sprouting from the lawn as I stood there in disbelief trying to grasp what was happening. Then walks up this perky, cute twentysomething. Oh, crap. This prepubescent male would be sleeping in the same bed as her. How do I stop this? Do I stop it? This had to be some sordid relationship. Or was it? Certainly, paying for one room would be a whole lot less expensive than two. Having the kid in the same room meant she would have a better idea of what he was up to. With it being a king bed, there was plenty of room not to have to touch the other person. Still, my gut told me something was not on the up and up with these two.

I showed them to their room. I was in a bit of a stupor and probably came across slightly ditzy. I was so perplexed by this twosome. I had no reason to deny them access other than it felt wrong. Would Airbnb say that was reason enough to boot them out? What if I got the police involved? Was a crime being committed and if so, what was it? Had the kid been sent to the door to throw me off? If so, it worked. I wanted to ask questions. All would have been offensive no matter the tone. Things like: Where the hell are your parents? If they are paying for your travels, then why not a place with two beds? I wanted the parents' phone number to call to check on the story. And if these two had permission to travel together, then what was I going to say? What was I going to do if the parents had no idea about the sleeping arrangement? I chose to be silent and cordial even in my awkwardness. Thank goodness it was for only one night.

Purposefully, I listened the best I could for sounds coming from their room that would indicate more than sleeping was taking place. Silence was all I heard. Good thing because the last thing I wanted to do was barge in. Of course, lack of noise does not mean nothing happened. I chose, though, to stick with my naïveté and believe they were merely babysitter and kid so I could sleep better. Despite my anxiety, I did not get any weird vibes from them, but the scenario still gave me the heebie-jeebies. My review said: "It would have been nice to know Nicole was showing up with a child. Both were nice to have."

I was not even bothered there was a child in the house. I do not think he was older than thirteen, the age Airbnb says is no longer a child. Even if he was thirteen, the scenario still hit a ten on the ick meter.

The Tahoe house seemed to attract questionable pairings. Another time two women showed up at the door, with one having my Airbnb page up on her phone. They informed me they brought a friend, and how my listing says it is zero dollars for a third person. What my listing also said is that only two people may stay. We argued at the front door. We were stern, but voices were not raised, and language remained civil. The woman/girl was still in the car. I acquiesced because I needed the money. Airbnb lets hosts refuse people at the door. I should have. I knew better than to let money be my default. Doing so has always backfired. Later, after calling Airbnb about the situation, the company provided me with a number in case a guest made me uncomfortable in the future.

After that experience I wrote on my listing that an additional person would be $300 a night, which was the maximum fee Airbnb allowed. Even though the listing said the space was for two people, there was essentially this loophole that this trio were using because there was no price set for an extra person. I never thought it would be an issue since I would only allow two people.

They were so good at pulling this off I am sure other hosts were scammed by them. Others had asked if a third person could come; usually a child even though the listing said no children. I even had people inquire about a third person sleeping on the couch. Essentially, it all amounted to them not being willing to pay for accommodations that truly met their needs, and instead wanting to shortchange me. This was not going to happen to me again. It is probably why I was so adamant about the woman in Mexico who essentially wanted me to create another sleeping area in the house because her sons would not sleep together. Going forward people got what they paid for and what each of the listings said.

The trio in Tahoe stayed three, long nights. There was an awkwardness the entire time. We all knew they swindled me. The third woman never spoke to me. I am not sure she knew any English. She was quiet, almost invisible. I wish I knew her story, too. Something was going on with this trio that seemed sketchy. I will never know if the silent one was there of her own free will. Their size would have made it easy for them all to sleep in the bed, so that was no big deal. What they did all day, well, I have no idea about that either. I only hope the young girl was not being used in some illegal manner.

It gave me pleasure to write an honest review that I hoped helped other hosts: "Stacy arrived with her friend and said she had another friend in the car. She had my listing on her phone when she knocked, showing me it said zero dollars for an extra person. Airbnb does not allow hosts to leave that category blank or to write N/A. The listing clearly states only 2 people. I let the three sleep together in the king bed. Then they left one (hour) after me and didn't lock the front door, so the house was open all day."

Writing the review did not erase the feeling of being used. I wish I would have reached out to the third woman, who really looked more like a girl, to see if she was OK. I will always regret that my anger toward the first two women prevented me from possibly seeing the third as someone who was in need of help. Was human trafficking happening right under my nose?

## Super Dirty

Cleaning house is one of my least favorite activities. Cleaning up after strangers took my dislike to a whole new level. Did people leave the room and house so messy knowing they had paid a cleaning fee? Did they not see the filth? Did they not care? Did people live like this just on vacation or was living in grime and disarray their norm at home as well? My stomach often turned on cleaning days in anticipation of what I might find. In Mexico, sometimes it was just one room that was messy, other times the entire house. Was it going to be gobs of hair on the bathroom floor and in the shower again, or a kitchen that looked like a mini tornado blew through, leaving food particles splattered on walls, floors, counters and appliances, or another used condom somewhere?

People paid a $50 cleaning fee in Mexico. I kept those dollars. In retrospect it would have been a better deal for me to have hired someone to clean the house, at least in terms of the value of my time. Based on how poorly people are paid in Mexico I would still have pocketed the bulk of that $50 after I paid a house cleaner. In 2022, the minimum wage in Mexico went up twenty-three percent to 172.87 pesos per day, or $8.50. That's per day, not per hour. In 2021, the daily minimum was 141.70 pesos, which in U.S. dollars is $6.97.

166

In Tahoe I did not add a cleaning fee until I had been renting the room for a few months. It started at $20, then increased to $35 near the December holidays, and was at $40 by the time I stopped being a host there. Cleaning in Tahoe was much easier because it was only one room and a bathroom. I cleaned the rest of the house before anyone came to stay, but it seldom needed cleaning after someone was there.

Bathrooms could be scary, especially after four people had been using the same one in Mexico. At both locations there were times when I could barely see myself in the mirror because it was so mucked up. I have no idea what that was all about. Even the large mirror in the Tahoe bedroom could be a mess. Whatever it was went beyond flecks of toothpaste and water droplets. Maybe I really do not want someone to explain how film builds up on mirrors, especially in such a short amount of time. The abundance of hair that covered bathroom floors and showers was atrocious. How could someone not see what they were standing on was a new color? It was their hair color. How hard would it have been to pick it up? It was disgusting. Maybe they did not care. The amount of hair was truly astonishing, especially when the stay was only a night or two. I wondered how much went down the drain, which led to the worry of needing a plumber. In Mexico the shower drain collected hair in a container just below the metal drain guard. I knew it was going to be gross when hair protruded out of the silver topper. The collection bin was always going to be slimy from soap, and sometimes filled with sand. The shower in Mexico was my least favorite thing to clean even without hairy guests.

A broom was near the front door so they could sweep during their stay. Clearly, most people did not use it on their last day. This would be akin to vacuuming before leaving. Not going to happen whether you are paying a cleaning fee or not. I would not do so as a guest, nor did I expect my guests to. Still, the amount of sand left behind was measurable at times. It was hard to see on the *Pulido* flooring, which is polished concrete. Unless they were walking barefoot, it would have been easy to not know the sand was there. The throw rugs in the bedrooms got shaken out after each visit; though, admittedly, it took me a while to realize this needed to be done. Considering the house did not have a vacuum this realization should have come a lot sooner. It was as if some guests had dumped a cup of sand on the rugs, spread it out and left it. I should have gotten rid of the rugs or at least suggested that to my sister. They were well-worn when I came along, and even worse by the time I left. Every room was swept in between guests, but not always mopped. I should have thoroughly cleaned the concrete floors in between each person, but I hated it, and I was terrible at it.

While I had extra linens, the laundry room was not accessible to me at the Todos Santos house once guests arrived. This meant everything needed to be washed, dried, folded and put away in between stays. Plenty of people line dry clothes in Baja, but that was not something I had ever done, nor did I want to start doing. I was grateful for the dryer because it was faster, and time could be a factor between guests. In Baja, quick turnovers were tricky because the house was bigger than what I had to clean in Tahoe, and more than one load of laundry was normal.

I never knew what the kitchen would be like. Sometimes it was a nightmare. The stove was often the worst, while some spills in the refrigerator became my nemesis. I could not believe the messes people left. I cannot go to bed without cleaning the kitchen first because I do not want to start my day doing dishes. Nor do I want to clean up a mess before I can start cooking again. I understand it was not a guest's job to clean, but I was truly surprised by the amount of grit they lived in even if it were for a short time. I would be embarrassed to leave a place the way some of them did, even with paying a cleaning fee. Apparently, the messy guests did not care they would be admonished about their level of cleanliness in a review. No one ever challenged me when I gave them a less than favorable rating in that category.

Dusting in Mexico always seemed pointless because of living on a dirt road. The big stuff got wiped down before people arrived, not necessarily after they left.

In Tahoe, it was rare that I did not jump on my cleaning duties as soon as people left. This mostly had to do with working as a journalist, so I never knew what any given day might be like. I was cognizant of when people checked in and out, and what my calendar looked like, so I knew how much time I had to clean. The good thing was that I did not have to immediately do laundry because I could access the machines while guests were in the house. I had extra sheets and towels (bath and hot tub), so if the laundry was not finished, it was not going to impact guests. It helped that I only had one room and one bathroom to clean. I always tried to vacuum the whole house before guests arrived, as well as spruce up the living room and kitchen. After all, they had access to the whole house and deserved to have the entire area clean. The coffee pot was in their room. This was always cleaned even if it looked like the guests had done so. Toilet paper was replenished. All the glasses were exchanged. Keeping the hot tub crystal clear was also a priority. Those chemicals could be mixing while I was working inside. Multitasking was necessary to get everything done. The Tahoe space was always easier to clean based on the square footage being so much less, no kitchen mess, and usually fewer people having been in the rental.

Sleeping wih Strangers

CHAPTER FOUR

# AJ the Co-host

## Making Bank

I have AJ to thank for being able to brag that my humble room in South Lake Tahoe was worth $500 for one night.

With her being in my profile picture for each listing, there was no hiding the fact I lived with a dog. I talked about her in each of my bios. I marked the box saying there was a dog on property. Reviews often mentioned her. For someone to be surprised about her presence was always mind-boggling to me. People showed up who were afraid of dogs, others were surprised to find dog hair in the house, and what startled me were the people who had no idea how to pet a dog.

AJ was a midsize dog who did not look threatening. At 35 pounds, most people could have wrestled her to the ground and dominated her. She was part greyhound, part yellow Labrador and other breeds I never knew. When I started Airbnb, she was 12 years old, with spunk, and a bit of an attitude. As she got older, she mellowed, became more of a love sponge, and definitely a beggar of attention and food with guests. She learned quickly who would feed her human snacks. She was definitely a shedder. I could have vacuumed every day and not picked up all her fur. It amazed me in Todos Santos how I would sweep, thinking I had all her hair corralled, only to turn around to find more to clean up. At times it was like I could create a small puppy out of all the blonde fur I collected. I wish I would have bought stock in lint rollers. The house was spotless, or so I thought, when I departed. Dog hair seemed to materialize out of thin air. It showed up without a dog being anywhere near the place. My sister was at the house eight months after we packed up and was still finding AJ hair. Knowing my dog was a shedder and that she slept on the bed with me, the comforter and shams in Tahoe got washed before guests slept on that bed. I then used a lint roller to get rid of any dog hair the washer and dryer did not remove. I did not want it to be obvious she slept on the bed when we were alone. With guests having their own sheets, hair was not an issue under the covers.

It was easy to tell if people were not dog lovers. One woman looked at AJ as though she were a wild animal about to pounce on her at any moment. She tried to put her husband closer to AJ as she practically hugged the wall to get to the room. This couple had booked the Tahoe room for five nights. It was going to be a long week with her not being a fan of AJ's. In situations like this AJ ended up being on the losing end because I would restrict her access in the house to avoid the guests. But this one time her presence paid off.

When I came home on their first full day, I noticed all their belongings were gone. No note, no text, no call, no communication through Airbnb. Everything had seemed fine other than the woman was not crazy about AJ. I was worried. What happened? Were they OK? Was there an emergency that called them home?

They did not respond to any of my inquiries. I was ghosted. Time passed. I contacted Airbnb to say I was worried about my guests who abruptly left. The key was back in the lockbox. Should I change the code? They had paid for four more nights. Maybe they would be back. Airbnb support staff got back to me after locating the missing guests. They were fine, just did not want to stay. Hmmm. The guy who booked the place finally emailed to say the woman could not stay another night with a dog.

It goes to show with couples that no matter the time they have been together each should weigh in about where they are going to stay. It seemed more the norm, though, for only the person who booked the rental to know what the place was going to be like and the rules that came with it. This was true for friends, romantic partners, and other pairings. It did not matter if a man or woman booked it. So many times the other person did not have a strong grasp of specifics about the accommodations.

I always wondered if this couple stayed in Tahoe the rest of the week. That was going to be an expensive proposition to pay for two places. What else was he clueless about before booking a five-night getaway? In my brief encounter with the non-dog lover, I got the feeling she was also the type who would not want to stay where the host was on-site. I am guessing they had multiple reasons for leaving. The guy never asked for a refund. I never offered to return the money. Because I had a rigid cancellation policy, he may not have wanted to broach the topic. Airbnb gives hosts a choice about cancellation policies. Mine was lax at one time. Then I had a last-minute cancellation which meant not getting paid. No one filled those nights and I had been counting on that cash. Then I changed the policy to be as restrictive as possible. In this case it meant $500 in my pocket for a one-night stay that was supposed to be five nights. I would have contemplated refunding his money if I could rebook the canceled nights. But I refused to be out money I was banking on.

I was not always a hard-ass. On another occasion people had to leave for a family emergency mid-visit. They took me up on my offer to let them come back within a year at no cost for the number of nights they had already paid. Another time a guy asked for a refund months in advance because his wife hurt her leg, so the ski vacation in Tahoe was not going to happen. I let them cancel with a full refund.

## Adjusting to People

While both Airbnb houses had fenced yards, AJ's access to them was quite different, which in turn resulted in her interaction with guests being different. In Tahoe she had the back yard to romp around in. If anyone joined her outside, they did so through the French doors. This was usually to get to the hot tub. A few people sat at the table, while others played badminton. This yard was primarily AJ's to do as she pleased. It was what I would consider a traditional backyard in California with gates on either side of the house and a fence enclosing the entire back yard.

In Todos Santos when I let her out of our room, she would romp down the stairs to go do her business or relax. She thought the gravel was a perfect place to lounge. Maybe it was a form of acupressure. The difference in fencing is that the entire property was enclosed, so the front, sides and back flowed into one another without obstruction. The front gravel area was also where everyone parked. The dog had two doors to test to see if she could get inside on the lower level; the front door, and the one that led to the lower-level patio. While I never spent much time downstairs even without Airbnb guests, when I did AJ was often with me. This meant she was super comfortable being inside on both levels. Even when the Airbnb section was not booked, laying on the front porch was common for AJ. The cool, painted concrete under the overhang was a favorite place for her to sprawl. It allowed her to keep an eye on the street, welcome anyone who arrived, and beat the heat of Baja. Rarely did she move for the guests, instead becoming an obstacle to step around. My apologies were met with total understanding from the dog lovers, and a shrug from others.

Being on the second floor, out of the way of the guests, I did not always know what she was up to. Begging for food and love? Obstructing their paths? Forgetting about her mom upstairs? She was fine. I was worrying needlessly.

In Todos Santos I also had to be cognizant of people closing the gate they drove or walked through to get to the property. Left open, she could roam. And she did. Early on she was a bit of an escape artist. AJ found gaps along the makeshift fence bordering the vacant lot. Just when I would plug one hole, she found another. Usually, she did not go far. It was like she wanted to explore a bit or take herself for a walk. One day, though, I could not find her. All the other times I could see her from the property. The gardener located her and led her back to her confines. Pepe offered a solution—weave bamboo stakes through the existing horizontal barbed wire to keep her inside the yard. That was money well spent.

Taking herself for a walk was a trait she brought south with her. In Tahoe she would go to a doggy day care on occasion when I was out of town, and she could not travel with me. I got a call saying she had escaped. The neighbors found her on my front step whining. Thank goodness she did not have to cross the highway

175

to get home. She must have memorized the route from the times we walked to and from the center. I never let her stay there again. If only she could have told me why she wanted out so bad.

Another concern in Mexico was that AJ would not move for vehicles. It was a warning I put on all the welcome emails to guests—"do not assume she will get out of the way when you pull in to park." That is why I tried to be around when people initially arrived, so I could keep an eye on the dog. It was also why sometimes I left her in the room instead of outside when it came close to arrival time for the guests in Mexico. In addition to not wanting her to be hit by a vehicle, I worried she would nonchalantly walk out the gate unbeknownst to the guests. Her well-being was my priority.

AJ became part of my family in August 2012 when she was nine. She was a rescue dog, so I have no idea what her life was like in the beginning. My friend, Joy, adopted her at an early age. The three of us went on walks in her neighborhood, to the dog park and sometimes other locales that might turn into a news story, like when we saw a questionable "control burn" near Fallen Leaf Lake or stumbled across all the graffiti at an underpass in town. AJ provided me with my dog fix after the death of my black Lab, Bailey. When Joy was diagnosed with cancer in fall 2011, one of the first conversations she had was to see if I would take care of AJ if the worst happened. "Absolutely," I said. For several months I was in denial that the conversation we had could become reality. When Joy died, I got custody of AJ, aka Audrey Jean. She was full of energy and a bit spastic, in some ways almost puppy-like with her exuberance. Through the years she slowed down dramatically, mellowed as it were. She lived to be nineteen.

She definitely had her quirks. She did not like men in sandals or flip flops, at least not in Tahoe. If only she could have told me where that idiosyncrasy came from and what it was about. I thought about asking guys not to wear those types of shoes but figured that would be a little over the top. Often AJ would nip at these men's toes. I innocently sloughed it off as though that was the first time she had ever done anything like that. Grabbing AJ's collar, I would lead her outside, away from the exposed male toes. She never did this to women. And she never did anything to the flip flops that were left near the front door. She only had an issue if a man was wearing them. Bare feet were not a problem for her. I kept her away from any flip-flop wearing guy she showed interest in just in case something super bad from her past triggered her to act in a manner that was actually threatening.

In Baja, it was rare for anyone to wear closed-toed shoes, so I was apprehensive at first not knowing what the dog might do. At the same time, her initial encounter with guests was so much different. This foot fetish showed itself in the entry way at Tahoe, a narrow space and just as we were all meeting. In Mexico, it was easier to keep her from guests unless she was in the yard when they arrived. Her initial introduction with people in Mexico was never indoors and never in tight quarters.

To get from our living area to her bathroom AJ had to go through the outside dining area in Todos Santos because the stairs were outside. This was a popular place for people to hang out. If she did not come back after a certain amount of time, I would go looking for her to make sure she was not in their way. She was usually in heaven. New hands to pet her and different human food to sample. Guests said she was not a bother, but I did not want her to be a pest. She was quick to sneak inside when their door opened. Multiple times I had to apologize for the four-legged visitor. She knew who she could do this with without it being a big deal. People often said they let her in, that she did not sneak in. Her instincts were spot on knowing who loved dogs and who would rather have nothing to do with her.

# Lover Dog

AJ had her own way of warming up to people. A group of four in Mexico did not mind that she made herself at home downstairs with them. After all, they were the ones who left the door open. Who knows what else was crawling or flying in. I chose not to point that out. This group noticed AJ was curious about them, but there was no tail wag that first night. By night two she was part of their family, tail wagging and getting petted. I had to retrieve her so she did not overstay her welcome. With another group on day one they were loving on AJ to the point she gave the woman kisses. That did not happen often, at least that I know of.

Most people shut the bedroom door in Tahoe when they left for the day or night. I suggested this so AJ would not go into their room. After all, she was accustomed to coming and going from every room as she pleased. Not everyone was going to be appreciative or understanding if she were in their room, let alone on the bed. The whole time we were in Tahoe she was nimble enough to get on the king-size bed, though eventually I provided assistance via a trunk at the end of the bed. This made the jump on and off the bed easier.

I have friends who managed to train their dogs to sleep at the end of the bed. This dog did not have that kind of training when she came into my life, and I did not try to instill it in her. AJ would use one of my pillows as though she truly knew what it was for. Sometimes she slept diagonally. No matter her directional choice it often meant having less room than if I were on a twin bed, when in reality I was on a king bed. Clearly, the dog was in control and we both knew it. When we were in the small Tahoe room it was the two of us on a twin bed. I had AJ sleep on the outside, while I was smashed against the wall. If someone came in, they were going to have to deal with her first. It might have been all in my head that she was some great watch dog, but to this day I would bet if I had been attacked, she would have at least tried to come to my rescue.

I was usually cognizant of her whereabouts. While working in the office she was a constant assistant as she laid behind my chair. If she got up, I figured she needed to go out. Depending on the weather, I would leave her out there a bit or wait for her to do her business. She never lingered long in the cold or snow. But the sun, well, that dog loved to work on her tan.

It never crossed my mind to tell people to close the door when they were in the room. I figured they could get AJ to leave easily enough if she were bothering them. What I never expected is that she would sleep with a guest even though sleeping was one of her favorite activities. She was as accustomed to being on a human bed as she was her own. I came home late one day to learn she took a nap with one of my single male guests on the king bed. He said she was great, just climbed right up and cuddled beside him. I can only imagine my expression was something like, "Oh, crap!" He quickly assured me it was all good. He did not even try to get her off the bed. Good thing because I did not know if she would growl at that suggestion. She would be telling this dude the bed was really hers even though he was paying to use it. He thought it was wonderful, and apparently AJ did too. I just looked at her incredulously and told her not to make it a habit.

What I never thought about before starting the whole Airbnb gig was if she might want to find another home. Several people loved on her so much I was worried she would want to leave with them.

# Non-Dog People

A couple of times questionable people essentially forced me to take AJ to my ex's for the length of their stay. I never figured out how to screen people so AJ would not have to stay somewhere else when Airbnb'ers showed up. I counted the minutes until those people checked out. I sent AJ away because I did not trust the people, not because I did not trust her. I had no idea if they would abuse her, taunt her, let her out intentionally or not care if she slipped past them as they came in the front door.

Dogs can sense when someone is scared, or when something is not right. People can be cruel. Even pushing her out of the way would be abuse by my definition. The non-dog person was not going to care if she was at the door wanting to go out, or at the door shivering to come in. It got so I could read the more responsible, caring guests who were going to be guardians for AJ when I was not home. Some of these non-dog lovers were upfront by saying they did not like dogs. Why they were even in my house was beyond me. They knew when they booked the room there was a dog living with me. They backed away from her in fear at the get-go and throughout their entire stay. All AJ wanted was love and to give some as well.

Admittedly, some of this was my fault. A couple from the United Kingdom wanted to come to the Tahoe place for two nights. He said his wife was uneasy with the thought of a dog in the house. My internal voice said, "Why are you even looking at places with dogs? Why aren't you listening to what your wife wants?" My email back said all would be fine. Again, there I went with putting money over common sense and the right thing. I have no good explanation for hitting the approve button. I should have put AJ first, but instead I saw dollar signs. Luckily, it worked out with no negative consequences. The whole time I am sure I was more nervous than the woman who does not like dogs.

When I knew a non-dog lover was on the property, I tried to keep AJ with me as much as I could. In Mexico I would go downstairs with her when she wanted out because I knew she tended to wander into the house, which probably would have freaked out the non-dog person. Others patted her in a motion that was not affectionate. They did not know to pet her with a long stroke from head to tail. It was more like a light, continual tap on the top of her head. I am not sure which one of us was more annoyed by this gesture.

## Other Dogs

I was surprised how many people wanted to bring their dog to Lake Tahoe knowing I had one. I even had a request from someone in Todos Santos. The listings said no dogs were allowed, so they already knew the answer. Maybe they thought they could convince me to break my rules like the people with children were able to do. I never allowed their dog to come no matter how well the people pleaded their case. AJ when she was younger did not like to share her space. She was good with other dogs, just not always in her home. She could get protective and snap at a dog in her territory. There was a time when she did not like other dogs to get near me. I am not sure if she was jealous or playing alpha dog or the behavior was rooted in her unknown past. Outside with the other canines all was good.

In her last year, she lived part-time with another dog in the house, so her anxiety was no longer an issue. But at the time of being my co-host I was never sure how she would react to another dog, and a stranger at that, in the house. No reason to test that situation. My sister was onboard with not wanting another dog on the property in Mexico, so the policy held in both locations.

AJ surprised me the most when in Mexico the dog sitter would come to stay the night with her dogs. They all got along. I swear that woman was some kind of dog whisperer.

Even if I did not have a dog, I am not sure I would have said yes to other dogs. Would they bark, pee inside, leave poop behind for me clean up outside? Plenty of dogs belonging to friends and family have stayed with me and will always be welcome. A stranger's animal was not something I wanted to deal with, especially since I was still getting used to human strangers in my home. Maybe their reviews would have convinced me to let their four-legged child come. Probably not, especially after my experience caving to people with two-legged kids.

Airbnb now allows hosts who welcome dogs to add a specific dog cleaning fee. After all, this type of surcharge is normal at hotels.

## The Bite

When I first got AJ she could be temperamental. As I mentioned, she was territorial with her space, with people getting close to me and with her monkey. In Tahoe I would throw that stuffed animal throughout the house for her to chase. She loved that monkey. Sometimes she would sleep with a paw over it as though she was hugging it. While she never aggressively snarled at me when I would grab it, she was vocal when strangers went for it. All they wanted to do was play with her. She did not care. That was her monkey, and she did not want them touching it. I quickly learned to tell people not to touch the monkey and all would be good.

In fact, one person mentioned the monkey in a review: "As a journalist she writes about walks and treks in the area and is incredibly knowledgeable about the places to go and see as she has been to them all. AJ has been to most of them as well and will make you feel very welcome as long as you leave (her) monkey alone."

AJ did not make a lot of noise. Barking was almost non-existent. Though, when I first got her, she seemed to hear things outside that were beyond my auditory spectrum. Or maybe she was smelling a wild animal. Whatever sense was triggered, it brought out the protector in her as she raced to the back door to scare off whatever might be there. Eventually she learned to sleep through the night.

AJ became such a sound sleeper that guests came into the Tahoe house long after we were asleep, and she did not budge. Nor did she make a peep. Even more alarming was that I slept through their arrival. People were being super quiet knowing we were in bed, but still, one would think I would not be able to sleep that soundly with strangers arriving late. This happened multiple times. Apparently, I got used to the whole Airbnb thing. Since I was not going to get up and welcome them, I might as well get a good night's sleep.

With AJ becoming more docile, I was more relaxed with her being around people we did not know. Letting my guard down was a bad idea. Letting a paid guest cuddle with her when she was in her bed backfired. AJ bit her on the lip. No medical attention was required. But I was rattled, as were the guests. I told all future guests when the dog was in her bed to leave her alone. That was her safe place. No more incidents after that. I wrestled with whether to mention the dog bite in my review. What would potential guests think? And who was at fault—the woman or the dog or me or some combination? Part of me wanted to get out in front of this in case she wrote something about the incident in her review. If I responded, I would sound defensive.

This is what I wrote: "An extremely nice couple. Unfortunately she had an incident with my dog. I didn't see what provoked it. I was surprise (sic) this happened because she is a third year vet student and she said she saw my dog's eyebrows furrow and ears go back, and yet stayed on the floor with the dog. They checked out while I wasn't there. I was sad to come home and see a hole in the wall where the front door handle had made a sizable indentation. One would have to throw the door open hard to have it damage the wall because there is a door stop there."

It was the damaged wall that pushed me over the edge. Maybe it was the dog bite that pushed them to slam doors.

## Canine Reviews

From guests' reviews it was as though the dog was the highlight of their trip. This is what some people had to say regarding AJ: "I think AJ might just be the kindest and most gentle dog I've ever met!" "We don't know what sounds her dog makes, because we didn't hear any. Very well behaved." "We were also greeted by her incredibly sweet dog AJ, who escorted us to our room." "AJ is a great dog to be company with, she is extremely quiet and friendly!!" "Thank you for the enjoyable stay and I'll miss AJ."

"You were right – AJ is a lovely companion." "PS – We love you AJ. You're supper (sic) sweet!!"

I even had guests write how they were disappointed they never met the dog. I wonder if I could have charged more just so people could have spent time with AJ.

"Walking inside, it was very warm and inviting, and her dog, AJ, was such a sweetie, greeting us at the door." "PS. AJ is the sweetest dog!" "Her dog, AJ, was very well mannered and incredibly sweet." "We liked Kae and AJ so much that we decided to extend our stay." "We received a bonus greeting from AJ her dog. What a bundle of love! Beware you'll fall in love with her!"

I also took note of how people treated AJ and said something when I reviewed them. Some of my comments were: "They were great with my dog, quiet and so easy to talk to." "Loved how they loved on my dog." "Great at making sure the gate was shut to keep my dog in." "They were quiet and respectful – even gave my dog treats and let her in as I asked." "I loved that Carla was concerned my dog had not been fed and was looking for her food when I arrived." "I loved how conscientious they were to make sure my dog did not get out." "They spoiled my dog with love."

Sleeping wih Strangers

CHAPTER FIVE

# Airbnb as Boss

## Communication from Above

As I have stated before, being an Airbnb host is a job. For the most part my interactions with the company were positive and timely. Still, it was disconcerting at other times to never have my concerns addressed. It was like calling the phone company when I have a problem; just put me in a line and eventually you will get to me, or not. I never felt part of a team. In many ways that was just fine; I like being my own boss. But the truth is they were my boss and should have been more responsive.

Fortunately, Airbnb through the years became more pro-active with communicating with hosts and guests via email. I received both once I fell into each category. These correspondences, though, were one sided. They did not solicit my feedback. One email sent to hosts said, "They clicked on your listing, then booked these places." This was about how Airbnb ultimately could make more money, and I might also. Even though this was not altruistic messaging on Airbnb's part, it was helpful because the information was free. Plus, I was not about to track daily visits to my listing. That would have been time consuming and possibly demoralizing. I would have loved to know why someone passed on my listing and picked another place. That level of detail was not provided.

Airbnb offered suggestions for what the nightly price should be, which could change daily. Their algorithm knows the listings surrounding your place and the prices that are being locked in. I never automatically went with their price selection because sometimes it was so low I would rather have an empty room or house than someone who would pay so little. Airbnb's price suggestions did not appear to take into consideration everything a listing offered. In Tahoe they wanted me to have a rate for my room that was the same as someone without a hot tub. In Mexico they did not appear to take the rooftop ocean view into consideration. Those amenities alone were worth jacking up the nightly fee. Not in Airbnb parlance, though. They just wanted the room booked. It was that simple.

One email that was of interest was titled: "How to promote your space on social media." The guy had more than one-hundred thousand Instagram followers. This got my attention because my sister who owned the Mexico house wanted an Instagram account for the Airbnb listing. While I had a personal Instagram account, I never put any effort into getting followers. I started the account for the Todos Santos house a week before I read the email. Having thirty-five followers in three days made me happy. Help with getting to one thousand, let alone one hundred times that number, would be welcome. Then I started reading the man's post. He partnered with a photographer who had more than two million Instagram followers. I stopped reading. I needed real world help with promotion. What they shared was not it. I would have been better off asking guests to promote the Airbnb listing on their social media pages; something like having them be influencers for my rental. My strategy was to post a picture every day to the Airbnb Instagram page with a ton of hashtags to lure people. No one who booked the place mentioned having seen the Instagram page. When I finally deleted that Instagram page it had two-hundred and six followers.

Another email from Airbnb came with the opportunity to offer discounts to guests based on certain available dates.

I said yes a handful of times while in Todos Santos. The company put a notice on my calendar about the price reduction so people perusing those dates would know. Airbnb also sent an email to people who had been looking at those dates but had not booked my house. Clearly, the amount of data the company collects is amazing and the ability to turn it into dollars impressive. No obvious reason why the discount worked on some dates and not others. One time Airbnb said the discount would be five percent and it ended up being eight percent. I never understood how that happened either.

While hosting in Tahoe, Airbnb offered to send a professional photographer to take pictures of my place. It was completely up to me which photos I used and the order I placed them. All but my cover photo were replaced by what the pro supplied. I kept the picture I took of the hot tub with wine glasses because this was a main selling point of my space and helped differentiate me from others. Now the company offers photography service in many locations, then deducts the cost from any income the host has earned until it is paid off.

Change is inevitable as a business grows, but the funkiness of the concept to sleep with strangers seemed to disappear in the time I was a host. Airbnb became a business where the big money-makers for the corporation were the stars and the rest of us were more like an afterthought. When I first started with Airbnb in South Lake Tahoe in 2015, I was invited to a gathering in town at a rental where Airbnb employees from San Francisco hosted us for a few hours. Much of the evening was spent talking to other hosts. This is when I first got a glimpse into how serious some people were about this being a primary business and not something to merely dabble in. Yes, I needed and wanted the money from Airbnb, but I clearly did not approach it with the gusto these people did. This was a full-time job for them. Airbnb's IPO filings stated ten percent of hosts were professional managers who created twenty-eight percent of the nights booked for the entire company. The employees gave a presentation about a promotional program to get more hosts. It sounded like a Ponzi scheme, with intricate financial incentives for getting new hosts. Why would I want more hosts in the town where I was a host? This would mean more options for guests and presumably less income for me. It was like cannibalism. Through the years Airbnb continued to offer incentives to people who signed up first-time hosts and guests. Compensation was credit to travel on their dime, not real cash. All credits came with an expiration date, and only one could be used per reservation.

One perk I benefited from was being a superhost. I achieved superhost status in Tahoe and Mexico. The company lets hosts know their status on a quarterly basis. The criteria for being a superhost includes having a certain number of reservations, at least a ninety percent response rate, no more than a one-percent cancellation rate, and maintaining a 4.8 overall rating. Considering less than ten percent of hosts achieve this designation, it proves attaining those goals is harder than it sounds. The reward for four consecutive quarters of being a superhost was a $100 Airbnb credit for travel. Of course it comes with an expiration date. Airbnb also adds a blurb to a superhost's listing explaining what this designation means and lists it as a category people can include in their searches.

## Pandemic Pivoting

Airbnb was slow to figure out what to do in 2020 when the COVID-19 pandemic hit. An outcry from hosts had them back-pedaling. They seemed to forget that without hosts, there would be no Airbnb. Instead of letting hosts know ahead of time or even "talking" to any of them, Airbnb sent an email with the policy changes. Even though in some ways the new protocols helped affected hosts, these were policies made without their input. A March 6, 2020, email talked about which reservations could be canceled without charges being incurred. I agreed with the decision. But I was also grateful to the hosts who let the folks in charge know that better communication was needed. From then on things changed for the better. Later that month the founders of Airbnb sent an email acknowledging the importance of hosts. They also explained why full refunds would be allowed, including the fees Airbnb collects.

By April 2020, Airbnb had set up a $17 million fund for superhosts who would need the money the most. Nothing was offered to all the other superhosts, let alone the bulk of hosts who are not superhosts. This all seemed discriminatory. The company chose the superhosts who received the $5,000 grant. This was not a loan because it did not have to be repaid. I was not one of the superhosts invited to apply for the cash. Airbnb chose the superhosts based on longevity with the company and "how badly their earnings have been impacted." I never understood how they would know how the loss of income would impact one person over another. I could only guess the biggest earners were the ones they believed were impacted the most. I disagreed with that assumption. Someone getting a couple hundred dollars a month on average might need that money to buy groceries. How were Airbnb decision makers to know a host's needs or how they used that money?

Another $250 million was available to help guests who had bookings that were canceled because of the pandemic. Those guests had the option to take cash or Airbnb credit. I had to cancel a May 2020 reservation in Berkeley, California, when my annual tennis camp with friends became a casualty of the pandemic. It did not take long for all the money to be reimbursed to my credit card. What irked me was the $70 Airbnb credit I used was lost forever per Airbnb's policy. That did not seem right considering the circumstances for the cancellation. My protest fell on deaf ears.

Even though I had guests cancel for a mid-March stay in Todos Santos because of the virus, I never received the partial reimbursement Airbnb said would be available. The guest reached out saying his brother who lived in the Seattle, Washington, area—one of the first COVID-19 hot spots in the United States—was not feeling well and they wanted to cancel. I understood and was even relieved they would not be coming considering the circumstances. At that early stage, so little was known about the virus. People were wiping down everything, including groceries. I did not care if the guy was lying, though I have no reason to believe he was. I think people should be able to get their money back during a pandemic and when the travel is not necessary. However, at the time I could not cancel the reservation without it affecting my superhost status, so I told the guy how to proceed so he could cancel. It

192

all worked out. We had a great exchange through Airbnb's email platform; ultimately with him thanking me for how helpful I was.

In mid-April 2020, Airbnb turned off the instant booking feature in Mexico to comply with that government's regulations. I was surprised anyone would want to host strangers during the health crisis, let alone to not at least do some sort of screening beyond the minimum that the automatic feature provided. But then I never saw the pandemic as a hoax nor was I desperate for money. Airbnb continued to want people to open their homes to essential workers. I was not that generous. I would not want a stranger who was interacting with the public or a health care worker on the front lines to live with me in a temporary manner no matter how much money I could make. While I was not able to be a host at that time, I was supposed to be a co-host for a friend in the spring and summer of 2020. It was a situation much like what I had in my home in Tahoe. My friend pulled the plug on that idea as we shared the same fear of a stranger bringing the deadly virus into her home.

The company created cleaning protocols that were rolled out in May 2020. A handbook was created, and the company suggested leaving cleaning supplies for guests. Masks and social distancing were also encouraged. I doubt guests would know if a host had done anything different in terms of cleaning. The built-in extra time between bookings would make it easy to clean comforters, blankets and bulkier items that might not normally see a washing machine in between each guest, but who is to say that ever happened? While I applaud Airbnb for implementing extra cleaning protocols, the rules were arbitrary when enforcement did not exist. Airbnb does not have the resources to inspect listings.

Early in the pandemic, California and Nevada's governors issued stay-at-home orders. For the first two months of the pandemic, the city of South Lake Tahoe instituted a $1,000 fine for people violating that mandate. El Dorado County, which South Lake Tahoe is part of, in April 2020 issued a declaration that all non-full-time residents were not welcome in Tahoe. This later changed so second homeowners could stay at their properties. The Lake Tahoe Basin covers two states, five counties and one city. This makes it hard for locals to explain the differences and a nightmare for tourists trying to navigate conflicting regulations. That is true without an international health crisis. It got more confusing when Nevada lifted its pandemic restrictions sooner than California.

When COVID-19 numbers started to surge in late 2020, California's governor tightened the screws again. Travel to many locations, including Lake Tahoe, was to halt for three weeks, which included Christmas. By this time more people were doing what they wanted and not what the government or health care officials asked them to do. Airbnb at first listened to the people and not government officials by allowing hosts to book reservations. In December 2020, a headline in the *San Francisco Chronicle* read: "Airbnb is defying Tahoe's lockdown. Now, hosts and guests are left scrambling to make awkward calls." Five days later in the same newspaper was the headline: "Tahoe-area officials urge Airbnb to help halt rentals during coronavirus shutdown." Adam Thongsavat, Airbnb program director, had this to say in response to a letter from Tahoe area government officials seeking help: "... we are taking further action to support your efforts to discourage visitors from using short-term rentals, hotels, and alternative lodging during the current stay-at-home order. We recognize that with ski resorts remaining open during this period of time, there is

194

a unique demand for lodging in the Tahoe area." That was part of the craziness. Ski resorts were not closed, which only sent more conflicting messages to tourists and locals.

## Party Problems

When it comes to Airbnb in the news, the headlines at times are a marketing manager's nightmare. Like this one from the *San Francisco Chronicle*: "Orinda Airbnb Violence Fits Pattern—At Least 42 People Shot at Short-Term Rentals in Last 6 Months." The newspaper in that 2019 article reported how seventeen people died at Airbnb listings in a six-month span, with five of them being at the Orinda, California, house during a Halloween party. This incident had the San Francisco-based company scrambling to change its rules about house parties. The company responded to the Orinda shooting by saying it was going to verify all seven million listings in regard to accuracy of photos, addresses and listing details. Quality standards in terms of cleanliness, safety and basic amenities would be reviewed, and "those that meet our high expectations will be clearly labeled."

The whole Lake Tahoe region attracted plenty of people who wanted to party. Fortunately, no deaths occurred at a short-term rental while I was in the hosting business. City officials were slow to solve the problem which led to the voter-approved near total ban on short-term rentals. Plenty of people grew tired of calling the cops on short-term renters who were loud, noisy, and horrible neighbors. Airbnb on its website created a Neighborhood Support page where people could file a complaint for non-emergencies. Of course, those neighbors would have to know this was even an option. Airbnb was not going to send letters to neighbors telling them what to do.

The *New York Times* reported between March and October 2020 twenty-seven shootings had ties to Airbnb listings in the United States and Canada. The violence, according to the report, sprang from house parties. Host Compliance, a company that helps jurisdictions regulate short-term rentals, reported between July and September 2020 complaints about party houses soared two-hundred-and-fifty percent compared to 2019. These were for Airbnb, VRBO and other short-term rental listing sites.

As the violence continued because of house parties, Airbnb kept adding regulations. Beginning with New Year's Eve 2020, people without a string of positive reviews could no longer book a whole house for that one night to ring in the New Year. Another new rule was hosts younger than twenty-five had to have three positive reviews in order to book an entire house near where they lived.

A story titled "Airbnb Fights Its 'Party House Problem'" was in the *New York Times* in October 2020. These party houses were not limited to New York. They proliferated during the pandemic as people got tired of being cooped up, and not seeing friends and family. People took partying underground, out of the public's eye. Of course, that only lasted until the police got involved or complaints were made.

In June 2022, Airbnb permanently outlawed parties at rentals.

## Going Public

Financially, Airbnb flung from one side of the pendulum to the other in 2020. With travel coming to a screeching halt because of the novel coronavirus pandemic, the company let go nearly one-quarter of its employees. By December the company was on the road to recovery. In its initial public offering, shares were priced at $68; when the stock market closed on the first day of trading the price was $144. It meant the vacation rental business was worth more than $100 billion. This valuation was more than Marriott and Hilton combined at the time. In less than a week shares had fallen by twenty-five percent, meaning the three co-founders who became instant billionaires had lost $5 billion. Still, the three should be set for life. CEO Brian Chesky alone was worth $11.2 billion that first day.

It would have been nice if hosts could have gotten in on the early action, but that was not feasible considering there were more than four million of us. The real problem with giving hosts stock options was the federal laws dictating who is allowed to receive them. Hosts are not employees, so they were automatically left out. Even though Airbnb before the IPO put more than nine million shares into what it called a "host endowment" fund, it was not clear if all hosts would benefit from it. The value of the fund needed to reach $1 billion before the company would start spending it on hosts. Who would be given shares from that fund remained to be seen—would it be anyone who was a host at the time of the IPO or at the time the financial marker was achieved? I am not counting on receiving a single share.

Joe Gebbia, one of the co-founders of Airbnb, donated $25 million after the IPO to be divided between organizations working on homeless issues in the San Francisco area. More charitable acts are likely, at least from Chesky. He signed the Giving Pledge in 2016, which is an agreement to donate the bulk of his money during his lifetime. This is the endeavor created by Bill and Melinda Gates, and Warren Buffet.

# Questionable Policies

People do not always give much thought to their profile photo. They treat it more like social media than a business transaction. Airbnb did not mandate people have a profile picture, but a host could ask for one. If I were making the rules, photos would show the person's face, with only them in the frame. It could not be from Halloween or some party scene. It could not be their dog or some scenic photo. I would also mandate everyone have a legitimate photo of themselves verified by the company that hosts can see at least after the reservation is completed. As a host, it was reassuring when the photo online and the person at the door looked the same. At the very least it was a safety issue. Until writing this book I did not know I could have requested a photo from a guest or that Airbnb had the policy stating, "If a guest's profile photo doesn't include the guest's face and, for example, contains only a cartoon, an avatar, or a picture of something other than a person, you can cancel penalty-free by contacting Airbnb."

Like with most companies, policies and procedures at Airbnb changed through the years. Payment was the one that irked me the most. When I first started with Airbnb, money was in my bank account the morning after the first night of the guest's stay. Then it changed without notice. It got to where I had to wait until several days after the guest was gone to see the money in my bank account. This meant Airbnb was making money on what should have been my cash. There is no good excuse for this. It is not like the company was waiting to get paid before being able to pay hosts. The company had its money at the time the booking was made. Airbnb makes money off this pile of cash as it sits there before being distributed to its rightful owner. Even though Airbnb's website says payouts are usually distributed about twenty-four hours after a guest is scheduled to check-in, that was not the case for years. On December 5, 2019, the day after guests checked in, this email arrived from Airbnb, "We've issued you a payout of $466.08. This should arrive in your account by Dec. 11, 2019, taking into consideration weekends and holidays." This became the norm, where the money was not automatically deposited into my account until most guests were long gone.

Airbnb makes its money by charging a fee to guests and hosts. For guests it is usually less than fourteen percent, while for hosts three percent is common. Some short-term rental sites charge a fee for hosts to use the platform; not so for Airbnb.

People occasionally asked if I would rent to them outside the Airbnb portal. Not a chance. I was not losing much money in the big scheme of things, so financially it would not be a game changer to abandon the mothership. The biggest reason I stuck with Airbnb is the $1 million insurance policy it provided in case something bad happened. Bad could be damage to the house, someone hurting themselves or things I never wanted to imagine like a deadly house party. I never had to use it, but it was nice knowing the policy was there.

Most cities and counties in the U.S. collect a transient occupancy tax from short-term lodging like hotels. This is billed to the guests by the lodging property. Airbnb initially was reluctant to collect this fee on behalf of hosts, saying it was up to individual hosts to factor in the tax, and then reimburse their respective city or county. Hosts could not add a tax line to the online bill. It is easier for hosts and municipalities when Airbnb is the tax collector. The company acquiesced in some cases, but not all. The city of South Lake Tahoe collected the lodging tax quarterly from hosts; with bills sent to all those who had the appropriate permits.

A cottage industry that grew out of the accelerating short-term rental explosion was businesses specializing in tracking down non-permitted properties, collecting back taxes, with some offering code enforcement. Initially, this proved to be a better financial decision for many municipalities than having paid staff do the work. Once hosts were brought into compliance, it was easier to monitor them.

## Fighting Discrimination

After Airbnb launched its nondiscrimination policy in 2016, the nearly one and one-quarter million people who declined to accept the pledge were removed from the site. This included guests and hosts. A significant change that started that year was hosts did not see a guest's photo until after the reservation was made. The goal was to prevent hosts from declining a booking based on what a person looked like. This left names and verbiage in a profile that could potentially identify the person in some particular manner, which might lead to hosts discriminating against the would-be guest. The Airbnb platform at the time was available in sixty-two languages in one-hundred-and-ninety-one countries and eighty-one-thousand cities. With that amount of diversity comes the potential for discrimination by hosts and guests who are prone to that behavior.

When a host declines a booking, Airbnb asks why. The person had kids or too many people wanted to come at once were my usual reasons. This all went back to people not reading all the details on the listing. Lack of reading was another reason I did not want them. However, I doubt telling Airbnb they were non-readers who did not know the house rules would have sufficed. Canceling a reservation also comes with questions. Another positive regulation allowed hosts to ban guests of the opposite sex if they would be in the same living quarters. The friend I was going to co-host with did not allow men to rent her room by themselves. She did it for safety reasons.

The company came up with the automatic booking feature because hosts were accused of racially discriminating against potential guests. Discriminators presumably did not opt in to use the new tool. The convenience of it was amazing. Had I been using it while on my one-night get away in Tahoe, I would not have been so stressed about nearly losing a night's revenue when I did not have internet access. That incident was not enough to change my mind because with people sleeping a few feet from me, I wanted to know something about them through an email exchange. It did not seem like too much to ask to know who I was letting in before I passed them in the hallway of my home. With the scenarios being different in Mexico, the automatic booking was logical. Guests were downstairs and we were never in the same area unless it was outside. I was able to set up a few questions for them to answer as they finalized the reservation. I wanted to know if they had been to Todos Santos before, who else would be coming, when they expected to arrive, and the purpose of their visit. If they had the various verifications from Airbnb, they could book the house without me ever hitting the "approve" button. Automatic bookings sped up the process for everyone.

## Always Evolving

Clearly, since Airbnb's start in 2008 there have been significant changes. Some by natural necessity like revamping the website, how it can be used, and the various types of listings people offer. Then there were the forced and unanticipated changes. Those include adapting to violence, a worldwide pandemic, and towns that believed their character had changed because of the proliferation of short-term rentals.

One by one, communities throughout the world are implementing rules about how many short-term rentals are allowed, where they can be located, the minimum length of stays (with thirty days now a norm), as well as how many rentals a person can have in a given locale. South Lake Tahoe has one of the most restrictive ordinances in the greater Lake Tahoe-Truckee region. Voters in 2018 approved a measure to phase out vacation home rentals in most neighborhoods. Residents were fed up with the chaos vacationers brought to their neighborhoods through traffic, noise, garbage, and other nuisances. By the end of 2021 all permits for stays less than thirty days expired except in what is called the "tourist core area" of South Lake Tahoe. An ordinance affecting hosted rentals, like what I had in South Lake Tahoe, was approved in 2020. These types of rentals are still allowed in neighborhoods, but now with greater government oversight.

Airbnb continues to evolve into more than a platform for people to find a place to spend the night. It wants to be a full-service travel business. Through "experiences" anyone—not just hosts—could be a tour guide. It could be a tour of a city, taking people on a hike or being a guide on the ski slopes.

In 2022, Airbnb declared, "We are launching the biggest change to Airbnb in a decade." Airbnb Categories is designed to make it easier for guests to find hosts they might not otherwise have come across. Instead of merely putting in a location to search, the fifty-six categories dig deeper into what a person wants to do while traveling beyond the number of bedrooms and bathrooms required. An example the company used said, "So, if your Lake Tahoe home includes a chef's kitchen, the listing can appear in the Lake Category and the Chef's Kitchen Category—in addition to Lake Tahoe search results."

Another addition is Split Stay. Prior to this change someone would put in the dates they wanted to be gone and up came the hosts with calendars available for that entire period. While it is not always fun to pack up and move when on vacation, it can provide the opportunity to see different areas of a city or town. Plus, with the proliferation of remote workers since the pandemic, people may want a change of location. The four shores of Lake Tahoe are quite different, so being able to break up a stay would give guests a different perspective there. Todos Santos would be the same. Staying in town would be one experience, while being on the *otro lado*, where my sister's house was, would be quite different.

The third addition in 2022 was AirCover for guests. It provides them compensation if a host cancels within thirty days of check in, helps with finding a place if a dispute with a host cannot be resolved, and gives them resources if the stay is not as advertised. In this case my guests who stayed without central heat now would be able to contact Airbnb to have the company help find them another place or be issued a refund. AirCover for hosts provides $1 million in host damage protection and $1 million in host liability insurance. Airbnb already had a $1 million liability insurance policy for hosts that did not cost anything. This one is also free, but now includes pet damage, deep cleaning (such as smoke removal from cigarette smokers), and the need to cancel reservations because repairs need to be made from previous guests.

The only way for any company to stay viable and relevant is to continue to change for what it believes is the better. Airbnb has strived to do just that. It has three distinct groups to satisfy—trav-

203

elers, hosts, and the more than fourteen thousand people who get a paycheck from the company. Airbnb can no longer be considered a startup disrupter. It is a force to be reckoned with that has forever changed the lodging industry.

CHAPTER SIX

# No More Strangers

## They Said/I Said

"Review" might be the most overused word in this book. Early on I was obsessed with wanting a good review from guests. Reviews by guests and hosts are a selling point for everyone using Airbnb. I knew they would help me be successful. In turn my goal with reviews was to help future hosts know who I would welcome back and who to watch out for. I used those exact words time after time: "I would welcome them back" in my reviews. Cleanliness, quietness, and ease in communication were the three big reasons I would say that. Fortunately, no one ever wrote a horrible review about me or my listings. Any criticisms were constructive and accurate, like the lack of variety of cookware in Mexico and that there was dog hair in the Tahoe bedroom.

Below are some reviews from me to guests and from guests to me that have not already been included.

What I had to say about guests:

"A little more attention to detail would have been good, like not leaving the key in the front door and the door ajar."

"So quiet it was hard to know there were four of them."

"What a fun foursome. They were all wonderful. They left the house clean—even started their linens in the washer." (This was before the laundry area became off limits in Mexico.)

"What an honor to host her and her husband on their anniversary and only second night away from their infant. They were quiet, clean and just ideal guests."

"They were here for three nights for a music festival. Each night they got in after I was in bed. They were soooo quiet. The room was in great shape when they left. I would welcome them back any time."

"This might have been a first where I didn't ever meet a guest! Paul and I were passing in the night, so to speak. He was quiet when he came in after I was in bed. The room was practically spotless. I would welcome him back any time."

"The only issue is how hot they liked it in their room, having the thermostat in the 70s and one time in the 80s."

"What a fabulous couple. We didn't see much of each other because of the short stay and how active they were. I would welcome them back any time. They were great at telling me when they were going to arrive; updating me as they were a little later than originally planned. They were courteous in being quiet when arriving late and leaving early."

"He left the room spotless. I just wish we would have had more time to talk."

"They were out exploring the area more than they were at the house so we didn't get to interact much."

"It was great to see them having so much fun in Tahoe; as well as enjoying my house, hot tub and deck."

What guests had to say about their stay:

"I slept like a baby."

"If you need a place to stay with a local, it is definitely the place to be."

"I loved the little touches: the in-room coffee bar, the clean towels in the bathroom, and the very informative welcome binder with information for a ton of stuff to do and places to eat in Tahoe!"

"She knows everything there is to know about the area which made figuring out how to spend our week there a breeze. Needless to say the hot tub was phenomenal with the snowy weather. Overall it was an incredible trip and a large part of that was a result of an incredible host!"

"Kae and AJ were wonderful hosts. We carried conversations and exchanged bear/mountain lion stories."

"The room looks nicer than the picture and I had a great experience."

"The bed was huge and very comfy."

"We told Kae we were going to arrive at her place around 4am in the morning. She helped us with leaving the key in her lockbox. Kae left us with a detailed message so the check-in was no problem. We drove a Tesla and there was a wall connector 0.5 miles away from her place."

"Kae's place is located in a residential neighborhood, close enough to the main street to get food and to get to the parks, but quiet enough that we had no trouble falling asleep after a long day."

"This little gem in South Lake Tahoe was wonderful. Upon our departure, she told us the route to take to get the most out of our visit."

## Moving On

The question I hear most often is: "Would you be a host again?" "Doubtful" is my short answer. Airbnb as a company is not the reason I would not be a host. Overall, my experiences with the company were positive. What would get me back in the game is if I wanted to earn a few extra bucks, or perhaps if I ever have my own second home. Maybe if I am living alone when I am older, it would be an interesting way to have company for short bursts.

I never made that much money, which is one deterrent. Having more realistic goals would undoubtedly make a future hosting endeavor better. The most I netted was $11,211 in 2016 when I had forty-eight reservations that filled the room ninety nights. The greatest number of reservations I had—fifty—was my inaugural year when the house was available for the last eight months of 2015. If I had been a host the entire year, it may have been my best year financially. I finished 2015 making $8,259 with the house rented eighty-one nights.

Multiple variables come into play when comparing year-over-year statistics. The raw data does not include how many room nights were available each year, how many nights were at a higher rate because of a holiday, when there was a cleaning fee or not, as well as other factors to know truly what year was best in each category.

I believe one reason room nights and income dropped in Tahoe after the first year was because I had more competition. Airbnb was making a big push into the greater Lake Tahoe market. Guests had more options. This undoubtedly brought more money into Airbnb's coffers, and less cash into my bank account.

Being a short-term rental host is a business when it comes to the U.S. Internal Revenue Service. This was evident when filing taxes and figuring out deductions. In some ways it was like a home office. What percentage of the utility bill is related to the Airbnb gig, how much laundry detergent and water went to washing their linens? The list goes on and on as anyone who item-izes deductions knows.

While the positive comments from guests will always be something to hold onto, they are not enough to want to get into the hosting business again. At least not how I did it in Tahoe and Mexico. Once the Tahoe house became a vessel to make money via Airbnb, it never completely felt like my home. It was a revenue generator. In Mexico I was always a guest because others owned the house. This also meant I did not have the final say regarding what could be done. While both were great experiences, I do not miss sleeping with strangers.

# Acknowledgments

While a book has the author's name on it, so many other people are usually involved in making it a reality.

For starters, this book would not exist if three guys in San Francisco had not come up with the crazy idea that people would pay to sleep in other people's homes, even if it meant on a couch. A huge thank you to everyone at Airbnb who helped me while I was a host, and to those behind the scenes who continue to make the platform work every day for hosts and guests.

If it were not for all the guests who stayed with me, there would be no *Sleeping with Strangers*. Thank you for taking a chance on me and my rentals. So many of you made the experience incredibly enjoyable.

While the circumstances that led me to become a host in South Lake Tahoe were not enjoyable, I am thankful to my ex in so many ways. I know this book wasn't easy for you to read at times, but thank you for your input. You are one of my best friends and I think that says a lot about both of us.

Thank you to my sister and brother-in-law for allowing me to be a host at their Mexico house.

Thank you to my mom for helping with some of the finer nuances of the book.

Many people saw versions of the book before it went to print. Thank you Sue, Jill, Anne, Pam and Bridget for providing insightful feedback that helped to make it even better. A special shout out to Penny for another read when I thought I was already done.

Big thanks to Christel Hall for editing the book.

Joann Eisenbrandt has almost as much blood, sweat and tears in this book as I do. She is the creative genius behind the cover, and the woman who took my manuscript and turned it into a book.

www.ingramcontent.com/pod-product-compliance
Lightning Source LLC
Chambersburg PA
CBHW022051020426
42335CB00012B/638